BULIMIA

Book for Therapist and Client

Barbara G. Bauer, Ph.D.
Psychologist—Private Practice
Center for Family & Individual Counseling
Columbia, MO

Wayne P. Anderson, Ph.D.
Chair, Joint Training Program
Counseling Psychology
Professor of Psychology
Counseling Psychologist
Counseling Services
University of Missouri—Columbia

Robert W. Hyatt, M.D.
Private Practice in Internal Medicine
specializing in Adolescent Care
Columbia, MO

Contributions by **Margaret Flynn, Ph.D., R.D.**

ACCELERATED DEVELOPMENT INC.
Publishers
Muncie,   Indiana

BULIMIA
Book for Therapist and Client

Library of Congress Number: 85-72775

International Standard Book Number: 0-915202-56-5

Second Printing May 1986

Technical Development: Tanya Dalton
                          Judy McWilliams
                          Sheila Sheward

Cover Design: Sherry Palmer

Order additional copies from

Accelerated Development Inc.
Publishers   Tel (317) 284-7511
3400 Kilgore Avenue, Muncie, Indiana 47304

PREFACE

When first contacted to write this book, we were asked, "Can you write a book from which therapists can learn and also be one that they can share with the clients they see that have bulimia?" This seemed at first to be a formidable task however we agreed that such a book would be very helpful. Many times we had wished that we had reading material that we could give our clients, their parents, husbands, or siblings that explained bulimia, how it starts, why it persists, and also the process the individual could expect to go through in order to recover. Many of the books written for practitioners were very technically oriented, filled with research data and statistics. Those directed to the client were primarily descriptive in nature, giving a picture of what having bulimia was like but offering little beyond feelings of commonality with other sufferers.

The purpose of this book is to provide both pertinent information to practitioners dealing with clients who have bulimia and to be read by the clients themselves to demystify the treatment process and to give them a more complete understanding of their eating disorder. The hope is that the sharing of the information offered in this book between therapist and client will make treatment more effective and process of recovery occur more rapidly.

In addition to its dual approach to both therapist and client, this book is distinctive from other books on bulimia in another way. The authors of this book present bulimia as a multidimensional problem requiring a multidisciplinary team approach to treatment. This team consists of a psychologist or mental health worker, a physician, and a clinical dietitian.

For the psychologist, numerous specific suggestions for therapeutic interventions are presented that have proven to be helpful with our clients. Stages of therapy are discussed with suggestions made as to which issues are important to cover in each stage. Clients will be helped to understand some of the conflicting feelings that will arise as they reach the different stages. Family therapy and group therapy are considered to be so important that individual chapters are devoted to these topics.

This book contains a chapter detailing the medical complications and medical treatment approaches for the physician treating patients with bulimia. All members of the treatments team including the client need to be aware of these aspects of bulimia.

Because bulimia involves food and eating behaviors, as authors we felt the the inclusion of a chapter by a clinical dietitian would be especially important. Input about nutrition can be very meaningful to the client struggling with the fear of weight gain and lack of information about appropriate eating behavior.

The reader will find several chapters that provide information on aspects of dieting and food behavior that are necessary for understanding of the process of bulimia. These chapters explain how bulimia begins, why it persists, and why it is so difficult to give up. The authors examine the conflicting forces of societal influence and the body's natural physiology.

Both the theory and practice of treatment of bulimia are supported throughout the book by case histories selected from the authors' many years of experience. These case histories represent the stories of real individuals and have been altered only enough to disguise the client's identity. By reading the case examples, clients hopefully will feel less alone with their problems and gain encouragement from others who have felt like they do and have, through therapy, recovered from bulimia.

This is not intended as a self-help book, however, the authors' hope that individuals with bulimia, who choose the book to read, will gain encouragement to seek professional help to deal with their problems.

ACKNOWLEDGEMENTS

The authors would like to express their appreciation to the many clients who have contributed to this book. Several clients have read the manuscript in various stages of preparation and have offered additions and corrections that were very insightful. Other clients have contributed over the years by teaching us about their unique problems and have inspired us with their courage and persistence in overcoming bulimia.

ACKNOWLEDGMENTS

CONTENTS

6 PERSONALITY DYNAMICS **59**

7 EARLY STAGES OF TREATMENT **73**

INTRODUCTION

The case of Jan provides us with examples of many of the features of bulimia that we will be discussing in this book. We feel it provides an overview of the experiences and the attitudes of a fairly typical client who comes into counseling for the treatment of bulimic symptoms.

CASE OF JAN

As a high school student, Jan received many academic and extracurricular awards and graduated third in a class of 150. While in high school, she was active as an actress and enjoyed participating on the debate team. Until Jan got into junior high school, she was overweight. At that time, she weighed 170 pounds and stood 5'6" tall. She went on a very restrictive diet and in one year lost 62 pounds which brought her down to her present 108 pounds. Two years after the weight loss, at age 16, she started the binging and vomiting routine. She binges on sweets, ice cream, cookies, peanut butter, and candy as often as four times a day. She says that she has no feelings involved with the binging and does it as naturally as someone else might wash their hands. She has been binging and purging now for 4 years, vomiting after every meal. In the first interview, Jan expressed concern about the bulimia, about a feeling she had regarding problems in maintaining intimate relationships, and about being stuck in making progress in school work. She said she doesn't know who she is, she is working too hard to try to anticipate the needs of others, and she loses herself in the process.

She indicated that when she lived at home she was given many responsibilities: preparing meals, doing the laundry, house cleaning, and so forth, but she does not feel that these were unrealistic expectations for her family to have of her. The counselor, on the other hand, indicated that a more normal response would have been to complain about doing all of that work in addition to her full load of school work.

Highlights form the next five sessions with Jan show some of the usual features a counselor can expect to find in working with women with bulimia.

Session 2

Jan was very serious and task oriented today. She talked about how important her looks are in her relationships with others. People are not trustworthy and will only use you for what you can do for them. Feelings are shameful and dangers exist in expressing them to others. During the session she used a metaphor or having a "ball of hurt" in her stomach, "it's hungry."

Session 3

Today's theme was self-anger at her bulimia; "Why do I do this? Why did it happen? Look how I am hurting the people I care about." She spent most of the session crying. She talked about her early years, and says she had a perfect childhood up until the fifth grade when her mother became seriously ill and Jan had to take over much responsibility. She described herself as a perfect child who either got everything she wanted or knew how to get it by being the "good child." Jan can not remember ever being angry as a child. She says she gives constantly to others, but she finds it impossible to take from or let others do things for her.

Session 4

Jan started the session by talking about having had anxiety attacks for these last two weeks. Her description of these attacks included difficulty in breathing and swallowing and strong feelings of depression and hopelessness. Her discussion of how she protects others from her feelings by always appearing happy led to an outpouring of feelings: anger about the demands others place on her to always be happy, self-blame for bringing about rejection of herself by others, confusion because she doesn't want to be in school, fear because she doesn't know what she wants to do, and guilt because others seem to glide through school so much easier than she can.

Session 5

Jan feels pressed to make a decision to do something besides stay *in school. She does not know whether to go home, get a job, and so on. She is literally "sick and tired" of being responsible. To go home seems attractive to her because she could be dependent and be taken care of, but she expects that in reality the family will simply give her back all of her old responsibilities. Her parents are encouraging her to spend three weeks in a residential treatment center for bulimia.*

Session 6

Jan has solidified her plans to quit school and to enter a four week hospital bulimia treatment program. She wants to please her parents by succeeding in the hospital program and feels responsible for their happiness. Much of the session was spent clarifying lines of responsibility and consequent guilt, obligation, appeasement, and rebellion.

For counselors, clients like Jan have become common place. Almost unheard of 10 years ago, bulimia has become a major social concern. So much so that an explosion of articles and books on the topic has occurred (e.g., see the list of references at the end of this book). So many women are seeking treatment for this disorder that the first author, who is in private practice, sees almost exclusively women with bulimia as clients. The literature in the field often gives conflicting impressions as to what causes this behavior and how it can best be treated. We hear that it is mostly biological and the result of depression and that drugs are the best treatment. We hear that it is a behavioral problem and that behavior modification techniques work best. We are told it is an addiction and should be treated as such. Our own investigation of case records and reading of the literature shows that these solutions are not working. Yet, another look needs to be taken of causal factors and methods of treatment. Our experience is that treatment takes time and involves working on a wide variety of family attitudes, personal problems, and teaching ways of coping with feelings and stresses.

Client's portrayal of the overwhelmed feeling as she started therapy.

CHAPTER 1

EPIDEMIC OF THE 80s

The authors who work in three different settings have been impressed with the marked increase in recent years of clients with eating disorders. We have been at self-help meetings for persons with eating disorders where as many as 150 have attended, some frantic with fear because their behavior was out of control, and others disturbed because they were being asked to change behavior which they saw no need to modify. The extent of the problem nation wide is difficult to measure, partly because of different opinions as to the definition of an eating disorder. If we use periodic binging or gorging on food as a criteria, estimates are that as many as 67% of the female population have an eating disorder (Polivy & Herman, 1985). With a more restrictive definition Halmi, Falk, and Schwartz (1981) found that 13% of their sample of college students had all the major symptoms of bulimia. Of the 13% who reported symptoms of bulimia, 87% were women. Even if we are cautious and take the most conservative estimations in the literature as to the extent of this problem, 4% of college aged women are victims. This means that the number of people who are suffering from this disorder is still very large.

What is Bulimia?

In this book we will use the definition for bulimia developed by the American Psychiatric Association and published in the Diagnostic and Statistical Manual of Mental Disorders (third edition) in 1980. Their criteria for bulimia:

A. Recurrent episodes of binge eating (rapid consumption of a large amount of food in a discrete period of time, usually less than two hours).

B. At least three of the following:

1. consumption of high-caloric, easily ingested food during a binge

2. inconspicuous eating during a binge

3. termination of such eating episodes by abdominal pain, sleep, social interruption, or self-induced vomiting

4. repeated attempts to lose weight by severely restrictive diets, self-induced vomiting, or use of cathartics or diuretics

5. frequent weight fluctuations greater than ten pounds due to alternating binges and fasts

C. Awareness that the eating pattern is abnormal and fear of not being able to stop eating voluntarily.

D. Depressed mood and self-deprecating thoughts following eating binges.

E. The bulimic episodes are not due to Anorexia Nervosa or any known physical disorder.

Almost unheard of 10 years ago, bulimia has become a major social concern; so much so that an explosion of articles and books on the topic has occurred (e.g., see the list of references at the end of this book). So many women are seeking treatment for this disorder that the first author, who is in private practice, sees almost exclusively women with bulimia. The literature in the field often gives conflicting impressions as to the cause of this behavior and how it can best be treated. One group of authors tells us that bulimia is mostly caused by biologically based depression, probably genetically inherited, and that psychoactive drugs are the best treatment. Another group of writers defends the position that bulimia is a behavioral problem and that behavior modification will work best in curing it. Still others believe that bulimia is an addiction and should be treated as such. Our own experience based on work with our clients, investigation of case records, and study of the literature suggests that none of these explanations are complete in and of themselves. We feel another more integrative look needs to be taken at those factors that cause bulimia and at those treatment methods that produce long term changes in client behavior. In this book these issues are presented so therapists will gain guidance in dealing with clients with bulimia, but in addition it is written so that clients can read it to gain more knowledge about themselves and the treatment process.

What Causes Bulimia?

Three major factors underlie our theory of why people develop bulimia:

1. *The stress in our culture on weight control.* In writing this book we have come to the conclusion that perhaps the disorder we should be trying to cure is America's preoccupation with dieting. As a nation we have become almost schizophrenic in our treatment of food. Our ads encourage

people to eat, we have richness of choice, the prices are cheap in comparison with other nations, we are, in short, a nation where becoming overweight is easy. Within seconds of being enticed to eat we can be confronted with the dangers of overweight, or with encouragement to be slim. The encouragement is coupled with a new diet or a new pill to relieve hunger. This worship of thinness is a major factor in creating bulimia.

2. *The cognitive control of the body's natural need for food is limited in most people.* People with anorexia may be an exception, but people with bulimia are not. The semi-starvation diets on which women with bulimia place themselves lead to problems with the innate control mechanisms which attempt to keep body weight within certain limits. When the cognitive controls break down bulimic behavior results.

3. *Not all people will feel the need to push their physical limits to the same extent.* A certain type of personality and temperment, inherited perhaps from the family, will need to be present. The personalities of these individuals will have developed in the context of certain family and social structures. Those individuals who have the appropriate (inappropriate?) personality characteristics and who wish to be thin will be risking development of bulimic behavior.

All three of these factors must be present to some extent for the condition to develop. In the following chapters we will explore at some length these three factors. More importantly we present a structure for treatment with concrete suggestions of how to handle both the general problems these clients present to the therapist and the specific problems that arise with special cases. Our solutions are not easy ones to apply, and we have found no magic road to helping these clients. Our experience is that treatment takes time and involves working on a wide variety of family attitudes, and personal problems and necessitates teaching clients (patients) more effective ways of coping with their feelings and the stresses in their lives.

The case of Jane provides us with examples of many of the features of bulimia that we will be discussing in this book. We feel this case provides an overview of experiences and attitudes of a fairly typical client who seeks therapy for the treatment of bulimic symptoms.

Case of Jane

Jane comes from a family of professionals. Her father has a Ph.D. in biochemistry and her mother is working on her Ph.D. in the same field. Jane has completed a bachelors degree in geology and is considering graduate school.

Jane is the middle child of three children. She was born just ten months after her older sister. From the time she was little, Jane can remember being told she came too soon after her sister was born and how hard this was on her mother. She remembers feeling guilty over this as a little girl and wondering if she was wanted in her family. She states that her mother was always very occupied with her sister who was very timid and had some minor health problems and that her brother was "Dad's boy" but that she never felt that she fit into the family very well.

Jane describes her mother as being very rational and intellectual. "I can never remember being hugged by my mother. She showed her caring by doing things for us like driving car pools and cooking." Her father was very distant. "He did not become involved with me until high school when I became anorexic."

Jane remembers her eating disorder as starting during the second year of high school. She returned to school after the summer vacation and saw the coach for whom she had run track the previous year. He made a comment that she wouldn't be able to run as fast this year since she had put on a few pounds over the summer. Jane was crushed by his remark and vowed to diet. She continued to lose weight until she reached 89 pounds. She was hospitalized by the family's pediatrician on a general pediatrics ward. No therapy was done. Her weight was restored to 100 pounds and she was released. For the next two years, Jane alternately gained and dieted with her weight fluctuating by ten or more pounds.

Jane developed bulimia when she went to college. She reports feeling very pressured by the work load in college and the emphasis on weight and attractiveness that was so prevalent in the sorority to which she belonged. She began self-induced vomiting in an attempt to lose five pounds. Jane thought she could stop vomiting at any time and was shocked to find that she could not break the cycle on her own.

When she first came to this therapist, Jane was vomiting 2 to 3 times a day. She rarely binged on large amounts of food but could not tolerate even a normal meal in her stomach. She used no laxatives, diuretics, diet pills, or other drugs. She exercised by running two miles three times a week. Her weight had stabilized at 105. She was 5'2" tall. Jane reported difficulty getting to sleep at night and had developed the habit of drinking one to two shots of whiskey to help her fall asleep.

Session 2. Jane talked about her feelings toward her family. Last Christmas, her sister talked to the family on the phone and announced that she no longer wished to be contacted by them. She has not been in contact with them since that time. We discussed the anger someone must feel to literally divorce her family. Jane cried and stated how hurt she was by this and how she felt she must make up for the hurt her sister caused her parents and be as good as possible so that she would not hurt them too.

Session 3. Today Jane talked about her relationships with men. She commented that she always seemed to lose herself in the relationship. When asked what she meant,

Jane explained that she becomes so busy trying to be exactly what she thinks her boyfriend wants her to be that she loses touch with any wants or needs she may have. Jane has a pattern of dating men who are very demanding and critical. Her current boyfriend knows of her bulimia and attempts to "help" Jane by threatening her, physically restraining her after eating, and telling her how much her behavior upsets him.

Session 4. Jane came in depressed today. She was teary-eyed from the beginning of the session and sat slumped in her chair. She could not identify a cause for her sadness but said she had been feeling very down for several days. The therapist asked Jane to describe the physical sensations in her body that were connected with the depression. "It is an emptiness inside like catacombs—winding and dark and not leading anywhere." The therapist had her close her eyes and go into the catacombs and try to find the part that was hurting. She reported it was like when she was growing up and her mother was not there for her. The therapist instructed her to light a candle in the catacombs and find the child. When she had done this she was encouraged to comfort the child, tell her that she loved her, and slowly lead her to a safe place where there was sunlight and warmth. The therapist told Jane that she was now the caring adult she had always needed as a little girl. When Jane opened her eyes, she reported feeling very tired but calm and no longer sad.

Session 5. Jane wanted to talk about her future today. She realizes that she has never made a career decision for herself. "I majored in journalism first because that's what my boyfriend in high school went into. I switched to geology because that is what my next boyfriend was majoring in. Lately I have been leaning toward chemistry but I think I am just following my parents now." The therapist asked Jane about past experiences she remembered as pleasurable and rewarding. Jane described two things with obvious enthusiasm: when she had spent a semester working in a pre-school and when she had volunteered as an aid in a nursing home. It was pointed out that both of these activities involved much interaction with people. Jane stated the appreciation and acceptance by the children and nursing home residents made her feel very good about herself. Arrangement was made for Jane to take vocational interest tests.

Session 6. Jane reported having a difficult week with her roommate. The roommate's boyfriend had moved in with them without Jane's permission. Jane stated that she did not like having him there but felt guilty because she was unhappy with the situation. The therapist and Jane discussed her need to please everyone at all times. This lead to a discussion of how uncomfortable Jane is with both her own anger and the feeling that someone is angry at her. Jane and the therapist discussed several alternative ways she might approach the roommate with her dissatisfaction.

For Whom Is This
Book Intended?

For therapists, clients like Jane have become common place. By taking a broad view on causes and treatment from the points of view of psychology, medicine, and nutrition we hope that we can help professionals working in this area increase their ability to help individuals with this disorder. We also have written this book with intelligent lay readers in mind so that clients, their parents, and spouses can read it with profit. This book is not intended, however, as a self-help manual, and we encourage individuals with eating disorders to seek professional help.

Do Men Have Bulimia?

Up to this point in our discussion we have been referring to him and her, however, in the rest of the book whenever we are discussing bulimia we will refer to she/her. In the studies which are cited in this book, the reader will soon find that women are primarily the ones who develop symptoms of bulimia. Overall, the estimate is that women make up 90 to 95% of the population with this disorder. As we discuss the pressures in this culture for women to be thin and the personality dynamics of the families from which these women come, one can more clearly understand why women are the primary victims. Men with similar backgrounds usually respond with a different set of problems, drug abuse, workaholism, or perhaps excessive exercise.

In summary the disorder of bulimia, which strikes mainly young women, is on the rise. Besides the cultural and family factors which primarily influence women, we will look at a number of other general factors such as biological and emotional factors which play a role in the development of this disorder. Therapy issues and stages will be described including specific techniques the therapist might use and the clients' reactions and role in the therapy process.

CHAPTER 2

MEDICAL ASPECTS OF BULIMIA

The aim of the current chapter is to acquaint the reader with the clinical syndrome, medical complications, and medical treatment of bulimia. *The evaluation of a client with an eating disorder should involve a multidisciplinary team approach.* This should include a mental health professional to assess psychological and family status, and to provide individual, group, and family therapy as indicated. The team also should include a dietitian to evaluate nutritional status and needs and to offer assistance in establishing optimum nutrition to the patient and her family. Involvement of a health care provider, usually a physician or a physician-nurse team is necessary for appraisal of medical status, evaluation of complications, and direction of appropriate medical therapy.

A physician's or health care provider's first contact with a client with an eating disorder will probably stem from one or more medical complications. Most of the medical complications of bulimia result from behaviors practiced by the individual with the intention of losing weight or avoiding weight gain, including intentional malnourishment, binge eating, self-induced vomiting, cathartic abuse (emetic or laxative), diuretic abuse, and strenuous exercise. Since the client will not usually volunteer that she has an eating disorder, or associate the medical problem as a complication of bulimia, the physician or health care provider must be aware of the clinical conditions characteristic of bulimic syndrome when obtaining a medical history. Those behaviors which result in the medical complications of bulimia are directed at weight control. Only by specifically questioning the client about her methods of weight control is the physician or health care provider likely to appreciate the etiology and clinical significance of her chief medical complaint.

The following two case histories are presented as examples of the difficulties that can develop when a physician is not informed about the existence of bulimia in the patient.

Case of Sherri

Sherri is a 38 year old white female who had been bulimic for 25 years. At age 18, Sherri reported that she had been very thin, giving a history consistent with anorexia nervosa. At the same time, Sherri stated that she had been addicted to amphetamines, taking far more than the prescribed dosage. She had been a beauty pageant contestant and had won several of the competitions.

Because she was experiencing palpitations and had suffered multiple syncopal episodes (loss of consciousness), she was referred to a cardiologist. He diagnosed her to have mitral valve prolapse and placed her on two antiarrhythmic medications. At the insistence of her psychologist, Sherri told her cardiologist about her bulimia, specifically that she vomited frequently and occasionally used laxatives. However, the cardiologist did not feel that this was clinically significant and did not pursue the topic.

Sherri was encouraged to seek further medical consultation and was eventually diagnosed to have hypokalemia (low serum potassium) related to her bulimia. Correction of this by liquid potassium supplement improved her symptomatology. An important note is that, prior to seeking psychological help for depression, Sherri never had considered her eating behavior problematic. She never had thought of herself as having bulimia and resisted accepting the diagnosis for some time even though she was informed that she had all of the symptoms.

Case of Karen

Karen is a 20 year old college student and the daughter of a physician. Karen was seen at the student health service at her college complaining of weakness and fatigue. Physical examination was unrevealing. A routine blood test revealed hypokalemia (low serum potassium). Because of this abnormal laboratory finding, Karen was evaluated extensively for adrenal dysfunction and concern was expressed regarding possible excessive licorice ingestion (both causes of low serum potassium). Only after Karen returned home for the summer did her father become suspicious and confronted her with the knowledge that he had heard her throwing up and knew she had bulimia. Karen was very ashamed of the bulimia but admitted to having the disorder when her father confronted her.

In addition to the hypokalemia, a careful medical history by the physician at the student health center would have revealed several near syncopal episodes (loss of consciousness), amenorrhea (loss of menstrual cycle), and weight loss. All of these findings would have pointed to the probability of bulimia as the etiology for the low serum potassium, avoiding the need for further diagnostic tests.

What Are the Demographic Features?

Demographically, a typical client with bulimia has been described as a woman with a mean age of 23.5 years (range 18 to 35 years), unmarried (71.4%), from an upper social class (77.1%), and in school (57.1%) (Fairborn & Cooper, 1984). Unless specifically questioned, the client may fail to give a history of binge eating or self-induced vomiting. Since the great majority of bulimic women are at normal body weight, the fact may not be appreciated that she has a high probability of exhibiting morbid fear of fatness (85.7%), extreme awareness and sensitivity to weight gain (55.2%), disparagement of body image (28.6%), or pursues a pathological goal of weight loss (22.9%). Although many individuals with anorexia nervosa practice many of the weight loss efforts described here, they are distinguished from those with a diagnosis of bulimia by the presence of severe weight loss (greater than 25% of normal body weight).

Binge eating is the primary identifying feature of bulimia (Russell, 1979). Binges usually take place when the individual is alone. The woman generally consumes large amounts of food high in carbohydrate, easily swallowed, and selectively textured. Reports have been made that as many as 50,000 calories may be consumed by one individual in several binge/purge cycles during the course of a single day (Mitchell, Pyle, & Eckert, 1981). The average size of a typical binge is around 3500 calories but may be repeated several times a day. The most common way of ending the binge episode is self-induced vomiting.

Evidence of the binges may be well hidden. Care is taken to avoid the appearance of binging in the presence of other people. For example, the woman may go from one fast-food restaurant to another, ordering a moderate amount of food at each stop. College students who eat meals in the dormitories may go back to the food line for several refills but return to different seats each time so that they will not be observed eating by the same people. After awhile, the individual may avoid eating with others entirely. She may become uncomfortable with even a "normal" sized meal in her stomach and feel the immediate need to rid herself of the calories. Repeated trips to the bathroom immediately and ritually after eating may raise suspicion of a problem.

In addition to avoidance of eating with others and excuses to use the bathroom during and after eating, several other clues exist with which family and friends may become concerned. Rapid fluctuations in weight, often of ten or more pounds, hint at binges and purges. Noting that a person eats a lot of food but remains about the same weight or actually loses may be indicative of bulimia. A common occurrence is for parents or friends to call their family physician and ask if they should be concerned about these behaviors.

What Is the Clinical Syndrome?

Women with bulimia who practice frequent vomiting often complain that they fill up during or after a meal following consumption of a relatively small amount of food. This characteristic is referred to as early satiety. Physiological studies have been done which show delay in the emptying of the stomach (Saleh & Lebwohl, 1980). Patients with bulimia report food remaining in their stomachs for several hours rather than the half hour to an hour experienced by a normal individual. Existent is a retraining of the stomach's normal mobility and a reversal of normal forward wave function. Spontaneous regurgitation of food may occur.

Most women with bulimia report that induction of vomiting becomes progressively easier the more they practice it and with some, the vomiting begins to occur without having to be induced. Weight control may also be attempted by the use of *laxatives, emetics,* or *diuretics.* In one study (Fairburn & Cooper, 1984), 31.4% of bulimic women used laxatives at a rate of 28.1 occasions per month, with a mean use of 17.4 laxatives per occasion! Almost an equal number of women with bulimia spit out food to avoid absorption or exhibit spontaneous regurgitation of food. Diuretics may be added to the binge-purge behavior pattern to further attempt to control weight. Finally, a strenuous exercise program is common with the direct goal of burning off calories.

Depression may be obvious with solemnity, lack of motor movement, a slowness to respond, tearfulness, apathy, suicidal ideation, sleep disturbances, and general lack of evidence of pleasure or enthusiasm in life. The severity of depressive symptoms in bulimics are similar to those of patients with major depressive disorder (Fairburn & Cooper, 1984).

Similarities have been noted between the personalities of women with bulimia and women with *drug and alcohol abuse* problems (Hatsukami, Owen, Pyle, & Mitchell, 1982). Both were found to have similar MMPI (Minnesota Multiphasic Personality Inventory) profiles. Interestingly, 35.8% of the women with bulimia were excluded from the study because they indicated problems with alcohol or drugs. Nineteen percent had actually entered treatment for chemical abuse.

A careful *family history* will frequently be revealing: 29.4% of first degree relatives have received psychiatric treatment, most commonly for a depressive disorder, and 58.8% of first degree relatives have had a weight problem (Fairburn & Cooper, 1984). Not infrequently, the client herself will have previously sought psychological or psychiatric evaluation or treatment of the eating disorder; however, the physician encountering the medical complication of bulimia is not likely to be given this information. Secretive eating behavior is the norm, and outright deception may be encountered.

**What Are the Medical
Complications of Bulimia?**

The medical complications of bulimia result from the hazards accompanying intentional malnutrition, binge eating, self-induced vomiting, cathartic drug abuse, diuretic drug abuse, and strenuous exercise (Harris, 1983).

Intentional Malnutrition. Although *intentional malnutrition* is the hallmark of anorexia nervosa, intentional malnutrition represents a significant medical complication of bulimia in 20% of clients. The principle manifestations of malnutrition involve four body organ systems: endocrine, cardiovascular, renal (kidney), and gastrointestinal.

Malnutrition leads to disruption of normal hormonal secretion affecting the reproductive system. Clinically, malnutrition is most commonly manifested by the development of secondary amenorrhea (loss of menstrual periods), irregular menses, infertility, breast atrophy, and/or atrophic vaginitis. On rare occasions, clients may exhibit symptoms or signs of hypothyroidism including lack of energy, weakness, cold weather intolerance, dry skin, and brittle hair.

Malnutrition of severe degrees may seriously affect the cardiovascular system. Decreased cardiac muscle mass may lead to a low cardiac output, clinically resulting in low blood pressure and/or heart failure. Malnutrition also may result in a severe deficiency of dietary potassium. Hypokalemia (low serum potassium) commonly results in cardiac dysrhythmias, and if severe, may lead to sudden death.

Hypokalemia (low serum potassium) accompanying malnutrition also will adversely affect the renal and gastrointestinal systems. Hypokalemia results in a specific injury to the kidney tubules, affecting their ability to concentrate urine. The resulting clinical manifestations are polyuria (frequent urination), nocturia (frequent nocturnal urination), and polydipsia (increased thirst). Hypokalemia also results in decreased gastrointestinal motility. The resulting physiological manifestations are delayed gastric (stomach) emptying and decreased gut motility. The resulting clinical manifestations are gastric fullness, regurgitation of food, reflux esophagitis (heart burn), constipation, and exacerbation of external hemorrhoids.

Binge Eating. This is a behavior which commonly results in medical complications. The principle body system involved is the gastrointestinal tract. Binge eating produces acute gastric dilitation, clinically manifested as abdominal distention, abdominal pain, nausea and vomiting, and rarely, gastric rupture. Post-binge pancreatitis also has been reported; the etiology for inflammation of the pancreas is unclear, but results in a devastating, life-threatening illness. Binge eating also has been reported to lead to a variety of nonspecific neurological symptoms, including headache, dizziness, paresthesias (numbness and tingling of the fingers and toes), epilepsy, and perceptual disorders.

Self-induced Vomiting. This behavior accounts for most of the common physical manifestations of the eating disorder and several of the life-threatening complications. Self-induced vomiting adversely affects four body organ systems: the alimentary tract, the pulmonary system (lungs), the renal system (kidneys), and the heart.

Self-induced vomiting has adverse affects on five components of the alimentary tract: the oral cavity, the teeth, the parotid glands, the esophagus, and the stomach. Lacerations or contusions to the oral cavity (throat) result from the insertion of fingers or foreign objects to induce vomiting. The presence of gastric acid in the oral cavity produces dissolution of tooth enamel; the clinical presentation is that of increased sensitivity of teeth, increased numbers of dental caries, and pyorrhea (gum infections) (Wolcott, Yager, & Gordon, 1984).

Bilateral parotid gland enlargement may occur. The parotid glands are those at the angle of the jaw that typically swell during mumps. The enlargement of these glands results in a round face or "chipmunk cheeks" appearance.

Reflux of gastric acid into the esophagus from either self-induced vomiting or chronic relaxation of the lower esophageal sphincter will result in esophagitis; clinical manifestations include dysphagia (difficulty swallowing), odynophagia (pain on swallowing), and rarely, esophageal rupture. The latter complication is a severe, life-threatening problem, with a high mortality rate. Self-induced vomiting may lead to gastric (stomach) atony or decreased motility, resulting in delayed gastric emptying. The latter may clinically present as gastric obstruction or lead to delayed absorption of drugs (including cathartics).

Self-induced vomiting may lead to aspiration of gastric fluid and contents. Aspiration into the tracheobronchial tree will result in irritation to those structures, clinically manifested by coughing. Aspiration into the lungs may produce a severe, life-threatening complication, aspiration pneumonia.

Frequent vomiting produces fluid, electrolyte, and acid-base disturbances. Loss of hydrochloric acid from the stomach results in the development of a metabolic alkalosis (alkaline blood). Metabolic alkalosis predisposes the kidneys to loose potassium. Potassium loss results in the development of hypokalemia (low serum potassium). Hypokalemia frequently accounts for the clinical symptoms of muscle weakness, decreased gut motility, decreased renal concentrating ability, and cardiac dysrhythmias. Excessive fluid loss by itself can lead to profound dehydration and shock.

Cathartic Drug Abuse. The fourth potential behavior directed at weight control is cathartic drug abuse which may affect three body organ systems: the heart, the kidneys, and the gastrointestinal system. Ipecac is a commonly available emetic prescribed by physicians to induce vomiting in patients who have ingested potentially toxic substances. Ipecac is usually not absorbed; however, in bulimic women with delayed gastric emptying, large doses of ipecac may be absorbed into the blood stream and produce toxic effects. Ipecac toxicity may produce lethal heart complications including dysrhythmias, conduction disturbances, and myocarditis. Clinically these cardiac complications may be manifested by irregular heart beats, skipped beats, syncope, chest pain, and shortness of breath.

The renal complications of cathartic drug abuse are those arising from the development of metabolic alkalosis, leading to hypokalemia and the renal disorder of impaired urinary concentrating ability. Laxative abuse also may directly result in severe potassium loss; stool is a rich source of potassium. Hypokalemia resulting from combined renal and stool losses can account for a variety of clinical manifestations, as previously discussed.

Chronic laxative abuse may produce several direct affects on the gastrointestinal tract. A functional bowel syndrome, clinically presenting as diarrhea alternating with constipation and abdominal pain is a common complication. The colon may be unable to conduct normal peristalsis, leading to "cathartic colon." Huge doses of cathartics are necessary to stimulate colonic motility; this finding probably accounts for the phenomenal tolerance for these drugs. Melanosis coli, a benign discoloration of the colonic mucosa, may result from the use of anthraquinone-containing laxatives. Finally, hypocalcemia (low serum calcium) may occur from gut malabsorption of calcium. Hypocalcemia, especially during concomitant metabolic alkalosis, can be clinically manifested by the development of carpo-pedal spasm (claw-like contraction of the hand) and tetany (involuntary muscle spasm and rigidity).

Diuretic Drug Abuse. Another behavior utilized by the bulimic woman to control weight is diuretic drug abuse. Although the principle complication is due to the renal loss of potassium via enhanced urine flow producing hypokalemia, the fact has been proven that diuretics can produce a large number of metabolic side effects. Less well known side effects include hyponatremia (low serum sodium), hyperuricemia (high serum uric acid), hypercalcemia (high serum calcium), hyperglycemia (high blood sugar), hypomagnesemia (low serum magnesium), hyper-triglyceridemia (high serum triglyceride), hypercholesterolemia (high serum cholesterol), and dehydration. Each of these metabolic complications may precipitate a clinical disorder or aggravate an existing disease. Discontinuation of abused diuretics frequently results in acute, transient fluid retention. Although the fluid retention is usually harmless, the cosmetic affect is poorly tolerated, and the diuretic abuse pattern is likely to be reinstituted.

Strenuous Exercise. The fifth behavior of women with bulimia is strenuous exercise which is directed at weight control by burning off calories. High levels of physical activity are often maintained even in the presence of malnutrition. Such women are especially prone to develop musculoskeletal problems (Rigotti, Nussbaum, Herzog, & Neer, 1984). Strenuous exercise also is well known to cause disturbances in reproductive function including delayed menarche, secondary amenorrhea, abnormal menstrual bleeding (e.g., erratic staining), and infertility. Weight loss, accompanying strenuous exercise, increases the incidence and frequency of these abnormalities (Bullen, Skrinar, Beitins, von Mering, Turnbull, & McArthur, 1985).

Two more case histories are presented to illustrate some of the diagnostic characteristics found in bulimia.

Case of Laurie

Laurie is a 24 year old female with Turner's syndrome. Laurie developed bulimia during her second year of college. She was followed by an endocrinologist for treatment of the hormonal deficiencies characteristic of Turner's syndrome. She was found to have an elevated alkaline phosphatase. Subsequent evaluation revealed slightly decreased bone mass and increased bone turnover. Laurie did not inform her physicians of her six year history of bulimia. She typically would vomit 2 to 3 times daily. She also reported early satiety and infrequent episodes of spontaneous post-prandial vomiting. When Laurie revealed her history of bulimia, the alkaline phosphatase elevation and decreased bone mass findings fit reports of bone loss related to eating disorders.

Laurie worked with a psychologist in both individual and group counseling and was able to resolve her many negative feelings about her body. Turner's syndrome results in a female with a short, squat body with a short neck. The women are also sterile. Laurie made many gains through counseling and decided that she was ready to phase out her binge/purge behavior. She made a sincere effort to retain moderate sized meals but reported that when the food was still present in her stomach several hours after eating, her restraint would break down and she would induce vomiting. She also experienced involuntary regurgitation of the food that she found unpleasant, which increased her desire to rid her body of the food. Laurie was placed on Reglan (metoclopramide) which resulted in a marked improvement in her gastric emptying and an elimination of involuntary regurgitation. Laurie continued taking the Reglan for 15 weeks and during that period stopped all binging and purging activity.

Case of Sharon

Sharon is a 23 year old secretary who was admitted to a psychiatric hospital for suicidal thoughts and plans. She had suffered from bulimia for 3 to 4 years. Sharon reported an average of 4 to 5 binge eating episodes per day followed by self-induced vomiting. She also attempted weight loss by taking 15 to 20 Correctol laxatives per day with subsequent diarrhea and dehydration. Sharon had documented hypertension but was taking not only her own prescription diuretics but also her father's antihypertensive diuretics (Metolazone and Chlorthalidone). She also had obtained Flexeril and Ativan which she took sporadically, usually in excess of recommended dosage. Sharon complained of fainting spells, shortness of breath, palpitations, epigastric pain, and paresthesias of face and hands. On exam, she had a blood pressure of 90/60 with orthostatic changes. Her heart rhythm was regular. Her potassium was 2.5 meq/l, indicative of a significant total body potassium deficiency.

Sharon was placed on oral potassium replacement of 15 to 40 cc per day of 10% KCL (20 to 25 meq/day). After approximately three *weeks of the supplement and no vomiting, laxatives, or diuretic abuse, her potassium gradually increased to 4.0 meq/l.*

What are Medical Treatments?

The intent of this section is to address only the more common medical interventions in the treatment of bulimia. Virtually all of the medical complications of bulimia can be avoided or reversed by cessation of the bulimic behavior. Unfortunately, the elimination of binge/purge behavior is often a slow process. Lecturing the individual about the dire consequences of her behavior is likely to have little effect on the eating pattern but will increase the individual's already strong sense of failure and guilt and will make her reluctant to return for follow-up. Maintaining a non-judgmental attitude is crucial when giving the patient factual information about her physical condition.

As illustrated by the case of Sharon presented previously, potassium replacement may be life-saving and prevent potentially dangerous arrhythmias. Patients need to be made aware that potassium is given as a treatment to reduce the chance of heart and muscle problems, even sudden death, and not as a *permission* to go on binging and vomiting.

The use of anticonvulsant medication in patients with bulimia is controversial. Initial reports indicated favorable results (Green & Rau, 1974); however, larger controlled series have found fewer of the subjects responsive to this form of treatment (Green & Rau, 1977; Wermuth, Davis, Hollister, & Stunkard, 1977).

The slow stomach emptying may be treated with drugs which speed the emptying process (Cohen, Woods, & Wyner, 1984; Alhibe & McCallum, 1983; Saleh & Lebwohl, 1980). The drugs used to speed stomach emptying are bethanecol (Urecholine) and the newer metochlopramide (Reglan). These drugs not only have effects resulting in more rapid stomach emptying, but also have central nervous system effects which may decrease binging and vomiting. The authors have found the use of metoclopramide to be of significant benefit when used along with psychological and nutritional counseling.

The patient may be very reluctant to accept this intervention. The thought that any food eaten will be digested and retained by her body is very threatening to the woman. This intervention should only be attempted when the individual has become ready to take responsibility for the amount of food she consumes. Consultation with other team members as to the timing of introducing this treatment is essential.

The use of antidepressants in the treatment of bulimia has been a controversial topic. Numerous studies have shown that many patients with bulimia are depressed. Many of these patients also have family members with affective disorder (Hudson, Pope, Jonas, & Yurgelun-Todd, 1983). However, one should note that many women with bulimia have problems with drug and alcohol addictions. Others have personality profiles similar to women with alcohol and drug abuse problems (Hatsukami, Owen, Pyle, & Mitchell, 1982). The high incidence of suicidal ideation and frequent history of suicide attempts is an additional consideration in the prescription of potentially lethal medication (Russell, 1979).

Many types of antidepressants have been tried with these patients. Two uncontrolled studies with small numbers of subjects have reported marked reduction of bulimic behavior with treatment with monoamine oxidase (MAO) inhibitors (Stewart, Walsh, Wright, Roose, & Glassman, 1984; Walsh, Stewart, Wright, Harrison, Roose, & Glassman, 1982). Caution must be used in the prescription of MAO inhibitors because of the necessity of dietary restrictions. Dietary indiscretion and impulsive behavior are characteristic of women with bulimia and many find they are unwilling or unable to eliminate the foods from their diet that could cause potentially dangerous reactions. Lithium, especially in those persons with a highly variable mood disorder (cyclothymic or bipolar mood disorder), has been found to be helpful in reducing binge/purge behavior (Hsu, 1984).

The largest number of patients have been treated with tricyclic antidepressants. In one report of a controlled study of 22 subjects, 90% of the women treated with imipramine displayed a moderate to marked reduction of binge eating (Pope, Hudson, Jonas, & Yergelun-Todd, 1983). However, in another study using amitriptyline combined with a brief behavior modification program, both the treatment group and the control group showed marked improvement (Mitchell & Groat, 1984). However, depressed subjects receiving only the minimal behavioral treatment program responded significantly less well than did non-depressed patients. Other reports conclude that "Our treatment experience with bulimics does not support the recent reports of successful treatment with medication alone" (Brotman, Herzog, & Woods, 1984, p. 7). Other authors have expressed the opinion that only patients exhibiting evidence of primary affective disorder or with severe depressive symptomatology should be treated with antidepressive medication (Mitchell, Hatsukami, Goff, Pyle, Eckert, & Davis, 1985).

Counseling should be started as soon as possible. Those individuals with few medical symptoms except binging and vomiting may well contact a psychologist as their first entry into the health care system. This places an obligation on the therapist to refer the patient for medical evaluation. The medical status and the presence of any physical complications should be determined before proceeding with psychotherapy.

In summary, medical treatment is an important part in a multidisciplinary approach to treatment of bulimia. Physical problems resulting from vomiting, laxative, emetic, or diuretic abuse must be treated. The use of drugs to stimulate gastric emptying may be appropriate as the patient recovers. Serious attention should be paid to the presence and appropriate treatment of depression concomitant with the eating disorder.

CHAPTER 3

INDIVIDUAL
DIFFERENCES

In this book, we will introduce a system which will account for many aspects of bulimic behavior and give an explanation of how this behavior develops. Because of the complex ways factors interact to produce any particular reaction, to decide what is cause and what is effect often is difficult to do when we are dealing with human behavior. Thus, we recognize that what we are saying in this book will not apply equally to everyone who has an eating problem.

The treatment of some individuals with eating disorders may be complicated by additional psychiatric problems such as borderline personality disorders. The binge/purge pattern also may be occasionally present in schizophrenia. The treatment approaches discussed in this book are intended for individuals with bulimia uncomplicated by either borderline or schizophrenic systems. While the authors recognize the role of hospitalization in the recovery of many women, the thrust of this book is on outpatient management of bulimia. Even if hospitalization becomes necessary, topics covered in this book are relevant.

A constellation of factors occur with regularity in individuals with bulimia. However, be aware that the combination of physical and psychological factors which create an eating disorder come in different mixtures for different individuals and not all parts of the constellation will be present in every case. For example, inappropriate roles within the family may be very important as a causal factor for some persons; whereas, for others family relations may have relatively less influence and a history of being overweight may be the key variable. The therapist needs to adjust the focus of therapy to coincide with the unique features and combination in each case.

Does the Body Have a Self-regulator for Weight Control?

We will present data to support the theory that an individual's weight is, to a large degree, regulated by a biological system which exerts its control through mechanisms in the central nervous system. Because of normal variations, this set-point will be different from person to person, but because the set-point is under the control of the central nervous system, the range of weight within which an individual can function comfortably is limited. We find that this is a very difficult point for our clients to accept since the popular concept is that a person's weight is completely under her personal, conscious control. This belief is so strong that our clients refuse to accept the possibility that this set-point varies naturally from person to person. To understand the concept of set-point, one must recognize that weights of individuals vary along a normal curve, just as do other characteristics such as height. This concept reaffirms that a normal goal for one individual may not be appropriate for another individual.

A number of our clients with bulimia have read drafts of this book and found the sections on set-point very depressing. Their reaction has been, "Am I going to have to make a choice between having bulimia for the rest of my life or being fat?" Their fear of fat issues are brought to the foreground by this material. The reader who has bulimia needs to keep two concepts in mind when reading this. First, most individuals with bulimia do not need to gain much weight to get back within their normal weight limits. They will find that they have been spending a tremendous amount of time and energy and risking their health in order to keep sometimes as little as 5 pounds off. Second, as the reader will see, evidence is available to show that exercise and good nutrition can be used to help keep a person within reasonable limits. The problem in that last statement for women with bulimia is they may need to redefine the concept of what they need to look like in order to feel comfortable with themselves and acceptable to others. This redefinition must be based on reality principles not on current advertising and magazine models. We feel this redefinition can only occur as the individual becomes emotionally stable and secure in her own self-worth.

What Is the Set-point Concept?

The set-point concept regards the amount of adipose (fat) tissue each individual possesses as dependent upon a base line which is determined by factors which occur at several points during the individual's life. The central nervous system attempts to maintain or defend this set-point by making the individual feel hunger. As we will see, when these signals of hunger do not work to restore the individual to her proper set-point, other mechanisms are brought into play which can cause eating disorders in susceptible individuals. (For a more technical discussion of set-point see Chapter 14.) The personality factors that make some individuals more prone to developing eating disorders, especially bulimia, will be discussed in the section on family and individual dynamics. In this chapter, we will be focusing upon the biological influences which determine how much an individual should weigh.

What is a therapeutic weight loss for one person might actually be malnutrition for another. Woods, Decke, and Vasselli (1974) gave evidence that the mechanism of weight loss varies greatly among individuals. Someone who is obese because of heredity and/or early nutritional factors will have tremendous difficulty in losing weight and in maintaining that loss. A person who is heavy, on the other hand, as a result of weight gained for other reasons (e.g., pregnancy) will lose weight relatively easily and not have a strong tendency to go back to the heavy state once she has reduced.

Does Weight Vary from Person to Person as Height Does?

Accepting the concept that weight varies along a curve which is normally distributed means that to continue to think of most obese people as being pathological or weak willed may be technically wrong because being heavy may be a normal condition of their bodies. For this group of individuals to lose weight and attempt to keep it off would create a pathological condition of semi-starvation with its additional emotional and physical problems. Nisbett (1972) stated that many individuals in an "overweight" population may actually be "underweight" in terms of their natural set-point and may literally be starving all of the time. These people are fighting a battle with their biology that never relents. What normal weight persons probably do not appreciate enough is how much difficulty a person has who attempts to hold her weight below her body's normal set-point. This difficulty is true no matter how seriously the individual is committed to meeting cultural norms of slenderness.

Because of differences in Basal Metabolic Rate (BMR), the amount of food that the person eats may not be correlated with her actual weight. Research evidence gathered by Garrow (1978)and Wooley and Dyrenforth (1979) does not support the commonly held belief that overweight individuals generally consume more food than their leaner counterparts. Some heavy people may eat relatively little, and some slender people may be hearty eaters. In keeping with emphasis on individual differences, we recognize that even at the obese level some significant individual differences occur in eating patterns, and some overweight persons do consume large amounts of food. Brownell (1982) believed that obese persons may be cursed by a biology that prefers fattening foods and by a culture that provides unlimited access to these foods. We would add that other individuals may have been trained by their families to prefer fattening foods.

Does Binge Eating Occur Among People of Different Weight Levels?

Wardle and Beinart (1981) cited evidence from clinical studies that some form of binge eating is found in obese, normal weight, and underweight groups. The basic features of these binges are similar across all weight groups with the exception that most bingers do not purge or vomit. If you are fat and binge but not purge, this may be considered by most observers as normal and perhaps even appropriate. But if you are normal weight and binge and then purge, you are considered to have bulimia and your behavior is therefore abnormal. In actuality, these two conditions may be very similar in etiology and be equally emotionally damaging. Both may be aberrent behaviors which grow out of an individual's attempt to function at a level below her body's normal setpoint.

Before we get into a more elaborate discussion of how bulimia develops, the reader may be helped by reviewing some features of the disorder through reading intake case notes on three clients seen by three different therapists.

Case of Rita

Rita "confessed" last night to her parents that she has bulimia. She said she has been binging and purging (through finger induced vomiting) about seven times a week for over two years. She said the binge usually begins with her starting to eat a normal meal and then being unable to stop eating. Rita reported that she works as a waitress, and while on the job finds herself continually picking at the food; this picking then ends up with her going on to a full blown binge. She reported that she has been questioning if she wants to return to school for the winter semester since she found the fall semester so stressful. She believes she got under her usual 3.0 GPA.

Rita was brought to the counseling services by her father, and her reactions during the interview were such that I (as therapist) had the feeling that she does not have any strong motivation to stop this behavior at this time. Approval from people in authority such as myself and her father did seem to be a big issue for her. She also appears to be very perfectionistic and extremely achievement oriented. She seems very socially isolated and is somewhat fearful of dating or getting involved with others. Her parents appear to have a poor marriage. Her father also admitted that he too is a workaholic and that he has perhaps put too much pressure on his children to achieve. Rita is somewhat close to her mother, who also had bulimia as does Rita's younger sister. My impression is that Rita seems to be a very empty young girl who presently fills her life, literally with eating and vomiting. Her insight into her problem seemed poor as were her problem solving skills. Her emotions seemed somewhat shallow.

Case of Diane

Diane stated that she has had bulimia for two years. Recently she has become a born again Christian and has just been baptized. Members of her group who found out about the bulimia have persuaded her that giving up bulimia will serve as good "witness experience" some day. She said that most members of her family are heavy. She once weighed 141 pounds, but by dieting has been able to get down to 119. She now weighs 126 pounds and is 5'6" tall. She is well dressed and is definitely not what one would usually call "fat." However, she thinks that she is.

Her bulimic behavior consists of throwing up practically everything that she eats, which means that she has thrown up as many as 7 to 10 times a day. Her more usual pattern, however, is to vomit 4 times a day. She has never had to stick her hand down her throat since she found that her muscles voluntarily help her induce vomiting. She seldom gorges, just says she doesn't want anything in her stomach. At this time she does not seem particularly concerned about the bulimia but is mostly concerned with what may be wrong with her physically. She is complaining of fatigue, weakness, coldness, muscle pains, and a burning sensation in her throat.

Diane is very wise as to what constitutes symptoms and characteristics of bulimia. She knows all of the tricks of the trade and admits to loving her habit. Her background tells me (as therapist) that a good deal of stress has been in her family, and subsequently, she tends to carry a lot of the burden of the family's problems. Her primary reason for seeking counseling is her concern about her physical health—I feel she'll be sly and resistant to going beneath her surface issues. A lot of outside forces besides her own need for help led her to seek counseling.

Case of Karen

Karen stated she has a mild eating disorder. She has bulimic spells where she will binge/purge 2 to 3 times per day. She stated that these last 2, 3, or 4 days each and occur approximately 4 times per month. She reported that at her worst point she binged/purged 4 to 5 times per day. She also has used laxatives. These cycles began during her senior year in high school. At that same time her mother was diagnosed as suffering from depression by her psychiatrist and hospitalized. Her mother is currently taking medication. Karen said she is *angered by her father always placating her mother and would like to scream at her mother to get up and take control of her life. She described her mother as always seeming angry (she hypothesized this may be because her mother married early and had four children in quick session). Even when she and her siblings were young children, Karen stated that they had to clean the entire house when the other kids they knew only had to clean their own rooms before they could go out to play. Karen runs two miles per day and exercises in addition to her diet and her binge/purge cycle.*

Karen is resentful that she was unable to have the typical home life she feels her friends had and that she had no control over this. She is frightened by her lack of ability to control her eating in the same way that she attempts to control most other areas of her life. This need for control may be the result of her reaction to her mother's lack of control. To be in a situation she can not control seems very frightening to her.

CHAPTER 4

THE FANATICAL PURSUIT OF THINNESS

In recent years many of the women shown on TV, in movies, and in magazine ads have often been very slender, sometimes to the point of emaciation. These women are presented by the media as models of what is beautiful and attractive. For the average women to attempt to attain this level of thinness would be both difficult and unhealthy, because this model pays little or no attention to the natural build or set-point for weight of most normal women. This modern ideal is in marked contrast to the women that we see in many of the paintings of the old masters and to those women who were shown in ads and in the movies 30 years ago.

On the other hand, in terms of the unrealistic demands upon the individual women, and the resulting physical costs, the present standards of beauty may be more in keeping with the era at the turn of the century when women forced themselves to have a 20 inch waist by the use of a whale bone corset.

Is Thinness Becoming
more Fashionable?

While historically women's bodies have frequently fallen victim to dangerous or painful cultural standards of beauty, women with bulimia aggravate their problem by perceiving themselves to be larger than they really are. These clients almost always overestimate their true size (Williamson, Kelley, Davis, Ruggiero, & Blouin, 1985). This misperception confounds the whole issue, since they are not only trying to meet an unrealistic standard of beauty but their self-image is altered to the point that even if they approached this standard they might not be able to recognize that they had.

Recognizing that a shift in the ideal weight for women had taken place, Garner, Garfinkel, Schwartz, and Thompson (1980) sought to establish its extent in a more qualitative manner by looking at the changes that occurred over a recent 20 year period (1959-1978). They looked at the shape of Playboy playmates, Miss America Pageant Contestants, and the volume of diet articles in popular women's magazines. These authors first looked at the height-weight characteristics of the 240 Playboy playmates in that 20 year period. They found that the percentage of average weight for age and height decreased significantly over that time period. The drop in weight relative to height was especially marked over the last ten years studied suggesting that the process of the thinning of America has been speeded up.

The Miss America Pageant contestants were found to have dropped an average of .28 pound per year. When one considers that the winner has weighed significantly less than the average weight of the other contestants since 1970, validity is added to the premise that the ideal woman is thinner.

Is Dieting an Answer?

The increase in the number of diet articles published per year tells basically the same story. There is now much more preoccupation with weight loss as indicated by a significant increase in the number of articles on diets which have appeared in recent years in *Harpers Bazaar, Vogue, McCalls, Good Housekeeping, Ladies Home Journal,* and *Woman's Day.* A quick check of magazine stands will show the reader that new diets continuously are being presented to the public suggesting that the magic cure of last month is inoperative this month.

Many of these diets appear to be quite logical and one can see why a rational person who considers herself overweight would be willing to go on one of these diets. Illustrative of such diets are (1) the Weight Watchers All New Quick Start Diet, (2) 25 Tips from the Diet Center, (3) The Model's Diet; 47 Tips to Trick Off Pounds, (4) Dr. Lindner's No-Hunger Diet, (5) The Ladies Home Journal Togetherness Diet, and (6) Lose Weight Bite by Byte, the Personalized Just-for-You Computer Diet.

Interestingly, these new monthly creations continue to hold out hope that the dieters may yet find the "way," instead of suggesting to the readers that diets do not work on any long term basis. At this point the conclusion should be clear to any objective observer that permanent weight loss by following these, or any other diets, is an ephemeral goal.

But why, for many people, do new diets seem to be the answer to their excess pounds? As you read diets, you are struck by a number of assumptions that the writers are making. First, they assume that people should be thin. One diet goes so far as to claim that, "People have a right to be thin without being hungry." This assumption does not take into consideration the premise we are defending in this book, that people vary and that all people cannot be slender as defined by our culture. A second assumption the writers make is that if you have not lost and kept weight off, the reason is because you have not found the right diet. The diet they are pushing, of course, has the additional factor that makes it the right diet for you. Tied in with the second assumption is a third assumption, "Losing weight is difficult but anyone with sufficient will power can do it." This leaves people who fail feeling guilty and probably inadequate.

The people who prepare these diets do, in many cases, recognize that additional help is needed to stay on a diet and so a variety of suggestions are given to help the dieter increase his/her will power. Some suggestions are (1) carry an unflattering picture of yourself when overweight and look at it when you feel the urge to eat, (2) find a phone buddy you can call when the urge to binge strikes, (3) be sure to eat suggested snacks so that you never feel deprived, and (4) don't feel guilty if you break your diet. The dieter is instructed not to use the diet as an excuse to binge. Also, the dieter is to give credit to self for all the times he/she has stayed on the diet. We point out again to the reader that the tone of these presentations is reasonable and seductive. "Following our rules is the royal road to physical perfection." The weakness of their method is that they do not take into consideration set-point, emotional reactions to dieting, individual differences in what is normal weight, and unreasonableness of the media model. None of them say, "you may be a person who cannot find a diet that is perfect for you." And none of them admit that the goal a person has chosen as his/her ideal weight may be completely out of keeping with his/her biological needs and thus may actually lead to feelings of being physically miserable.

Some people, after trying a number of diets, do recognize that diets do not work for them, but they do not give up their pursuit of thinness. It is this group who provide a ready market for yet another set of magic roads to thin perfection by the use of diet pills, plastic wrappings, and electric stimulation devices.

American women, in general, seem to be preoccupied with weight. Huenemann, Shapiro, Hampton, and Mitchell (1966) found that up to 70% of high school girls were unhappy with their bodies and wanted to lose weight. As we have just pointed in our discussion of media influences, this desire to be thinner may be partly a result of societal models being held up as ideal. The media links being thin with "finding Mr. Right," "finding the perfect career," and "feeling proud of oneself."

Is Thinness Related to Social Class?

The concept of what an ideal weight should be also may be influenced by the mental connection many people make between being thin and being a member of a higher social class. This movement toward the thinner ideal shape is in opposition to the reality of a trend for American women to become heavier due to improved nutrition over the past 20 years. This places women in a conflict. We have a society which is on the one hand demanding that to be considered attractive a woman must have a slender figure, and on the other hand providing a nutritional level which causes women difficulty in achieving that shape. As a culture, we are caught in the bind of conditioning women to abhor their bodies and to strive to achieve a goal which is impossible for all but a few individuals who are naturally very thin.

Society does not tell us the goal of ideal thinness is a fantasy. Instead each magazine on the newsstand reinforces the fantasy by providing us with still another new diet. The message is that the goal can be achieved if only the right diet is found, the right behavioral modification system used, and the individual tries hard enough. If you do not succeed, the message from the media is that you are a person with a weak will and poor self-control. The conclusion reached is that losing weight and approaching the ideal means that one has self-control. Losing weight also means beauty, virtue, and higher social status. We conclude from the preceding statements that one factor in our search for the source of bulimia and the fear of fat is found in the current cultural norms which, while unfair to many of us, seem to have especially victimized our adolescent girls.

Has a Recent Evolution Occurred in the Ideal Body Shape of Women?

The preceding evidence supports the idea that a definite evolution has occurred in what is presented as the ideal body shape of women in our society over the last 20 years. We conclude based on the interest in diets and other weight loss programs, that the media ideal is being accepted as a goal by many women. Other factors, not yet recognized, also may be playing a role in the developing model of the very slender women as the attractive woman. Regardless of the source of the model, however, this new goal of thinness has been developing at the same time that the average woman's weight has been increasing. Thompson, Jarvie, Lahey, and Cureton (1982) cited a survey by the National Center of Health Statistics which provided evidence that American women now weigh an average of 13 pounds more than they did during the previous decade. The ideal presented to women in 1960 did not require them to lose much weight since the media model and reality were relatively close together. To look like the current media ideal, the average woman must lose a considerable amount of weight and thus function at a weight considerably below that which is natural for her. Our contention is that losing weight and attempting to maintain that weight loss puts many women in a state of semi-starvation, and this chronic hunger lays the groundwork for the development of the bulimic symptoms in women who also have the predisposing personality characteristics.

Is the Fear of Fat a
Major Factor in Bulimia?

Yes, an unreasonable fear of fat often does exist in those individuals who develop bulimic symptoms. The bias in this culture against overweight begins at an early age and is widespread. Brownell (1982) reported that, as early as six years of age, both thin and fat children find obese children less likeable than children who have gross physical handicaps. But while individuals who have physical handicaps are not thought of as being responsible for their condition, those who are obese are considered as having caused their obesity. Negative labels such as lazy, weak, and self-destructive are often applied to them. The use of these terms communicates quite clearly to the obese individual that he/she is personally responsible for a stigma which results in his/her being rejected. Given this strong negative message from the culture, one can easily understand why many of these individuals begin to dislike their bodies and become preoccupied with losing weight. In our experience, our clients who develop bulimia often have been teased by others about their overweight. "At 11, I weighed 160 pounds, and the other kids called me Miss Piggy. I become so upset with what I looked like that I dieted off 60 pounds in one year."

Case of Polly

Polly's story is a further illustration of this preoccupation with weight. At 5'3" and 108 pounds Polly would seem to be close to cultural ideal of weight to height. In spite of this, she is obsessed with her weight, particularly what she sees as poor distribution and too much weight on her hips and thighs. Polly engages in excessive exercise, for example, she does 960 sit-ups plus other exercises everyday. If she overeats, she will do her routine of exercises twice a day or more. She is a pleasant individual but when you talk with her you find she is totally preoccupied with thoughts of food. When she was younger, she was overweight (top weight 136 pounds). She stated that the worst thing in the world is to be overweight. Polly feels that the dangers of bulimia are worth the risk.

What Have Women with
Bulimia Said About Being Fat?

Several of our clients felt we were not stating our point on fear of fat strongly enough. One of them asked to add a comment. "If other people, (family and friends) are going to try to understand bulimia better after reading this, you must emphasize this point. We don't just have a violent reaction to going back to a previous weight, being fat is one of the worst things that can happen to you. I have never felt such a panic/grief like emotion, be it from divorce or death of a close relative, which is so intense as that evoked by the *fear of fat.*"

What Are Consequences
of Fear of Fat?

We are living at a time when the majority of adolescent females are very unhappy about their physical shape. This negative awareness causes them to be preoccupied with any sign of fat on their bodies. One group of adolescents, the one who are most likely to become clients with eating disorders, go a step further than the average teenager and become convinced that to be heavy (fat, obese) is catastrophic. To have "excess weight" becomes so threatening to their self-esteem that they see any method of bringing their weight into line with cultural expectations as acceptable. These women have a strong drive to appear thin, which we grant is not unusual for most women in our culture. But because of constitutional factors which we describe in Chapter 14 (set-point, genetic structure) and personality characteristics (perfectionism, need for control), they attempt to solve their need to be thin in an extreme fashion. This leads first to periods of excessive dieting and later to bouts of binging and in some cases purging.

This fear of becoming excessively "heavy" remains a central concern regardless of their success in lowering their weight. Russell (1979) discussed the course of this condition in his patients. He reported that they were nearly all struggling to maintain weight at a level which was significantly below an earlier weight level. He felt that the earlier level could be defined as their healthy weight even in those cases where the weight sometimes amounted to a slight degree of obesity. Their desire to reduce at first looked like a reasonable, normal reaction to their condition. When many of these women go on their weight reduction programs, however, they create a problem for themselves because they are attempting to force their bodies to function at what is an unnaturally low weight for them. Their bodies respond with a strong impulse to return to their predieting level of weight. They find that dieting is not working well for them, and a strong drive develops to eat more than average. As the dieters eat, they find themselves gaining weight on fewer calories than a normal weight person because of some changes which have taken place in their Basal Metabolic Rate.

In the case of the individual who develops bulimia, we find a rather standard pattern. Unable to maintain her desired weight by dieting, she soon becomes frustrated by her failure. Her attitudes toward losing weight become even more unreasonable. She then finds she has episodes of binge eating which cause her to turn to the methods of weight reduction characteristic of bulimia; vomiting, purging, fasting, or excessive exercising. Crisp (1981-1982) concluded that women with bulimia experience this as a loss of control over their appetite and body weight. This loss lowers self-esteem and makes them prone to periods of isolation. When they seek help from doctors, the purpose is to obtaining help in curbing their food intake so that they can arrive at their ideal weight. Russell (1979) stated that the problem "is clearly the patient's refusal to accept her constitutional weight that leads her to counteract the eating orgies by means of vomiting or purging or both." Russell (1979) was impressed with the strength of the negative reaction these women had when they were asked to think about going back to their original weight. Their original weight would not have made them truly obese, in fact in many cases, the extra weight would have amounted to very few extra pounds.

Case of Jan

One of our clients, Jan, provides a relatively routine example of what we have been discussing in this section. Jan has been preoccupied with her body image since she was a sophomore in high school when she began going on very restrictive diets. As a freshman at the university, she had read about bulimia and then heard that a high school coach had recommended throwing up as a way to control weight. At this time she started eating more and throwing up. She had been purging every day but shortly before coming into counseling had cut back to every other day. She exercised every day by running, lifting weights, and taking aerobic dancing. Jan had body image problems and thinks she is fat no matter how thin she is. She is very preoccupied with food and feels very guilty and embarrassed about this bulimia. She expressed the desire to be thinner and believed that she was not disciplined enough in her exercising and eating habits. She will not weigh herself but believes that she is constantly gaining weight. She seems to be very aware of how she is gaining a sense of control in her life by controlling the intake and rejection of food.

Does Dieting Generally Precede Bulimia?

In the previous section, we introduced the idea that a fairly long period of dieting usually precedes the onset of the bulimic symptoms. For most women who develop bulimia, a pattern of behavior exists which is consistent with the premise that long term dieting results in a state of semi-starvation. As a result of the constant hunger, the individual becomes very preoccupied with food. The weight loss, which was the result of the stringent dieting, can only be maintained by using very strong constraints on eating. Individuals who develop bulimic symptoms are evidently very good at staying on a diet. The available evidence suggests that about a year and a half lapses before their constraints begin to fail. Garfinkel, Moldofsky, and Garner (1980) found that, on those patients for whom he had available data, an average of 19.2 plus or minus 8 months passed after the individual began to diet for the binge/purge pattern to develop. Wardle (1980) also reported that strict dieting precedes binging and suggests that this may have a causal function. Boskind-Lodahl (1976) commented that "in each case, the young woman's effort to perfect herself through dieting had led to her first eating binge. After the binge came guilt, and after the guilt a renewed compulsion to lose weight either by fasting or purging."

Bruch (1973) found a similar progression in persons who became bulimic, that is, first the strict dieting and later an intense urge to gorge developing. Even the Japanese researchers Nogami and Yaban (cited in Wardle & Beinart, 1981) also found that the first symptom of bulimia was food restriction and only later did the binges occur.

In their study of 34 women with bulimia, Pyle, Mitchell, and Eckert (1981) found that 30 of them connected the onset of their bulimic behavior to a period of voluntary dieting. Many of these women had started to diet at the suggestion of a family member. An important added factor was noted in the Pyle et al. study in that 30 of the 34 patients recalled some traumatic event connected with the beginning of the binging behavior. The most common triggers were the loss or separation from some significant person in their life. Sexuality problems and arguments were also mentioned as triggers for binging behavior. We will discuss more fully the concept of triggers in a later section.

What Sequence of
Events Leads to Bulimia?

An examination of the case histories of our own clients supports the sequence of events outlined by the preceding writers. We see a number of common features in the cases of women who develop symptoms of bulimia; she is a woman who has perfectionistic standards, places a very high value on being slender, and goes on a restrictive diet. After a period of time on this diet, she becomes chronically hungry and develops an intense urge to eat. This urge can not always be successfully resisted, particularly if some emotional trauma is presented as a trigger. At some point the individual's control fails and she finds herself having an eating binge.

EFFECTS OF OVERCONTROL

Is the Need for Control
Frequent in Women with Bulimia?

Women who develop bulimia often seem to be striving for some mystic state of perfection. One of the ways in which they attempt to achieve this perfection is by always being in total control of their behavior. Again and again, as we read the case reports of other therapists, we are struck with the emphasis that these clients place on control: "She has begun to realize that the constant tension she feels stems from the rigid demands that she places upon herself." "She has a compelling drive to achieve in order to acquire recognition. To do this she insists on everything in her life being in order." The attitude expressed by these women seems to be that losing weight is just another situation where mind has to prevail over matter and that if their system of weight reduction fails, they just need to try harder. The amount of control that these women expect of themselves in order to keep their weight down would be seen as unreasonable by most people.

Crisp (1981-1982) discussed the idea that the almost universal teenage concern with weight control is part of their need to exercise internal restraints upon themselves in a world where society's indulgent standards are at odds with family expectations of restraint. The commercial aspect of our culture pushes self indulgence and emphasizes a consumer oriented, hedonistic approach to life. Ads encourage us to indulge ourselves, tell us that we "deserve a break today," that we should "go for the gusto." Middle class, achievement oriented families, on the other hand, promote values at odds with these outside norms. Crisp saw weight control as one way that these women bridge the gap which exists between these two powerful systems. Wardle and Beinart (1981) also believed that this strong need to have control of one's life leads to strict dieting followed by binge behavior.

Do Obese and Normal Weight Persons Differ in Response to Food?

Schachter (1971) found that obese and normal weight subjects differ with respect to their reaction to eating cues. Why is there this difference in response to food? Examining the data gathered in studies on the effects of semi-starvation leads to some tentative conclusions. The reader needs to keep in mind the evidence that has been presented to show that individuals who have bulimia are, in all probability, functioning at a weight that is below their natural set-point. This means that they are responding to their environment as if they were in a state of semi-starvation. These individuals think about food more than average, they are more likely to read articles on food preparation, and they are more conscious of food around them. This preoccupation with food will occur not only in obese persons who are attempting to lose weight, but also in anyone who is functioning at a weight which is below his/her own healthy level, whatever that level might be for him/her. Wardle and Beinart reported that some form of binge eating is found in obese, normal weight, and underweight groups and that the main features of binges, including onset after a period of strict dieting, are similar across all of the weight groups.

Are Binges Caused by Functioning Below the Normal Set-point?

Three variables are reported to cause binges in those individuals who are functioning below their normal set-point: emotional distress, alcohol, and preloads. A *preload* is the eating of some food which is normally on the individual's forbidden list or the eating of an amount of food that could be considered the losing of restraint or control over the diet. If we accept the possibility that a strong internal struggle is occurring within the individual, we can assume an approach-avoidance conflict about food. On one side are the need to be thin, the fear of fat, the need to be in control of their lives, and the search for perfection. On the other side is the need of the body to protect itself against starvation in the face of the stringent, unrealistic restraints which are being placed upon eating. These restraints upon eating in the face of what the central nervous system is responding to as semi-starvation, lead to some reactions within the person who develops bulimia which are different from those that we see in a person who is functioning close to his/her normal setpoint.

For example, Herman and Polivy (1975) found that anxiety in normal weight subjects caused them to eat less, resulting in loss of weight under stress. Individuals on a restrictive diet gained weight under the same conditions. In a subsequent article, these authors suggested that the emotional distress disrupts restraints on eating to which the dieter precariously adheres (Polivy & Herman, 1976).

Herman and his co-workers (e.g., Herman & Mack, 1975) developed a measure of dietary restraint, that is, a measure of the degree to which individuals feel a need to control their intake of food. This measure was a better predictor of how that person would behave toward food than was the individual's weight. Their findings are supportive of the view that it is the degree to which a person is functioning under his/her setpoint rather than his/her gross weight which causes the abnormal reaction to food.

The study which Herman and Mack designed to investigate this phenomenom was presented to subjects so that it appeared to be a taste test. In actuality, the set up was to measure the relationship between scores on the Restraint Questionnaire and amount of food eaten after being given either one or two cups of milkshake (the preload). Drinking the two cups of milkshake caused individuals who scored high in the restraint direction to eat more than if they had eaten only one milkshake. This reaction of eating more after they had been given more food to start with seems to support the idea that once their normal restraints on eating were overcome, they ate as if their controls were no longer functioning. Wardle and Beinart (1981) sum up their research on restraint by concluding that people who are on diets, regardless of how much they weigh are inclined to overeat after they have eaten food (a preload) which they believe contains a large number of calories. The individual's belief that her control has been broken or lost appears to be the important factor operating in this situation rather than the actual number of calories that she may have consumed.

Case of Vickie

> *The case of Vickie illustrates some of the factors which we have just been exploring. Vickie has been suffering from bulimia for 4 years and the condition fluctuates in intensity according to the amount of stress in her life; however, she is somewhat vague in describing just what these stressors are. The stressors seem to be mainly related to academic/work pressures and to her intense competitiveness, primarily with men. Vickie has a lot of anger toward her dead father because he was never around much. When he was alive, she had a lack of respect for him because she saw him as weak. The bulimia is part of her long-standing preoccupation with weight issues. Her mother was obese in college and lost 100 pounds. She conveyed her concerns about weight to Vickie and was determined not to let Vickie have the same problem. Partly in response to her mother's concerns, Vickie began a rather restricted diet and went from 135 pounds to 118 pounds (at 5'7''). At that point she found it difficult to maintain her weight, and after a year, she discovered, via information from a gymnastics coach, binging and vomiting.*
>
> *Vickie works at a restaurant which specializes in desserts. Vickie admits that this does not seem a particularly good place to work since sweets seem to precipate the bulimic behavior. She will take a part of one dessert, find that she lost control, and go into a binge. These binging episodes occur 2 to 3 times a day. She also has a problem with insomnia. This is partially related to drinking diet cokes as a food and energy substitute in the evening. She discussed with her counselor her tremendous needs for approval and the fear that she has that she might do something to offend someone and thus lose their respect.*

What Are some National Steps that Would Reduce Causes for Bulimia?

As our present emphasis on eating and dieting becomes more apparent, our equating of slenderness and beauty have given rise to a epidemic of bulimia. The authors hope that steps will be taken to moderate this situation. More public awareness should lead to more public education about the consequences of our present attitudes toward food and weight. We need more parent training which emphasizes good nutrition but does not lead to negative attitudes toward and teasing of overweight children. Boyfriends need to be reminded that their comments about weight can lead to problems. Schools need to shift the emphasis currently placed on team activities to teaching individual health and exercise programs that the students can take with them into their lives beyond school. Ad campaigns and TV shows need to have some overweight role models who are happy and who are attractive to others.

CHAPTER 5

EMOTIONAL RESPONSES
TO
DIETING

As we have worked with women with bulimia and studied the literature on the subject, we have found that depression is a frequent complaint. The question, which has perplexed us, is "Which comes first, the depression followed by eating problems or eating problems followed by depression?" While we feel that the preponderance of evidence that we are about to present supports the conclusion that depression is a reaction to the state of semi-starvation which develops after a long period on a restrictive diet. Considerable evidence exists that diagnosed depressive reactions tend to run in the families of individuals with bulimia (e.g., Hudson, Pope, Jonas, & Yurgelun-Todd, 1983; Strober, Salkin, Burroughs, & Morrell, 1982). This means that a predisposition toward depression may exist in these patients which is brought out or exacerbated by the restrictive diet.

Does a State of Semi-starvation and Dieting Produce Similar Behavioral Characteristics?

In terms of reactions to a number of variables, a great deal of similarity appears to exist between chronic dieters and individuals who are in a state of semi-starvation. To more fully understand the emotional state of individuals with bulimia, a review of the research conducted by Keys, Brozek, Henschel, Mickelsen, and Taylor (1950) would be helpful. They studied male volunteers who were put on a semi-starvation diet for a period of six months and whose behavior during that time was carefully monitored. These researchers found that the emotional consequences of semi-starvation were such symptoms as irritability, poor concentration, anxiety, depression, apathy, lability of mood, fatigue, and social isolation. In the subjects studied under those conditions, irritability was so marked and outbursts of temper so frequent that the group meetings which were a part of the program had to be stopped.

Brozek and Erickson (1948) studied the personality tests (the Minnesota Multiphasic Personality Inventory) of subjects who were on a semi-starvation diet. During the period before semi-starvation, only 3% of the subjects felt frequently downhearted. During the period of semi-starvation, this increased to 62%. The men in the study complained that life was a strain for them much of the time. The experimenters noted marked personality changes which they called a semi-starvation neurosis. They concluded that no fundamental differences between the kind of answers given by the semi-starved subjects and those given by patients with a clinical diagnosis of psychoneurosis could be found. As the experiment continued, scores obtained by these subjects increased significantly on scales 1 (Hypochondriasis), 2 (Depression) and 3 (Hysteria).

Are Personality Tests Scores Different for Women with Bulimia?

Two studies using the MMPI with women with bulimia found that their profiles also were markedly elevated. Williamson et al. (1985) found that women with bulimia had more psychopathology than did either normal or obese women. The group with bulimia scored significantly higher than did the other two groups on the same three scales 1, 2, and 3 as the semi-starvation group in the Keys study. In addition, the group with bulimia had higher elevations on 4 (Psychopathic Deviate) than both normals and obese and higher scores on 7 (Psychasthenia) and 8 (Schizophrenia) than the normal group.

These findings suggest that women with bulimia are more neurotic, depressed, impulsive, and manipulative than are either normal or obese women. Further support for these conclusions are found in a study by Hatsukami, Owen, Pyle, and Mitchell (1982) on the differences and similarities between women with bulimia and women with alcohol or drug abuse problems. They also found significantly elevated scores on scales 2, 4, 7, and 8. These women tended to be overanxious, have difficulty making decisions and have difficulty with interpersonal relations. In our own study of clients with high 2, 4, 7, and 8 MMPI profiles, family problems and low self-esteem also were major presenting problems (Anderson & Bauer, 1985). All of this would indicate that along with all of the other symptoms that we have just mentioned that depression is a prominent feature in the MMPI profiles of women with bulimia.

The studies just mentioned were based on tests given after the eating disorder had developed. They do not tell us if the pathology was caused by the eating disorder, caused the eating disorder, or if both were caused by some other combination of factors. Other evidence is needed if we are to make sense of these findings. If we look at other studies of the reactions of individuals who are on a self-induced diet regimen, we find that they also have many of the same kinds of emotional problems characteristic of people who are on a semi-starvation diet. Nogami and Yabana (cited in Wardle & Beinart, 1981), in their study of 16 patients who were on restrictive diets, found that those patients' symptoms also included depression, aggression, low self-esteem, and dependency.

Are Suicide Attempts
Common Among Women
with Bulimia?

Nisbett (1972) found that the most commonly reported symptoms of individuals, functioning below their biological set-points for weight, included depression and irritability with some reports of more serious problems such as psychosis and suicide attempts. Thoughts of suicide are common among our clients and other writers frequently report suicide attempts by clients with bulimia. Russell (1979) found that 11 of his 30 (36%) clients had attempted suicide, in Pope and Hudsons' (1984) sample 47 out of 136 (35%), and in Garfinkels and Garner's (1982) group 19%.

What Are the Symptoms
Associated with Loss
of Weight?

In a study done by Crisp (1981-1982), 119 subjects had at least three of the following symptoms in connection with their loss of weight: anxiety, depression, anxiety associated with meals, increased interest in food and food preparation, feelings of being cold, constipation, and amenorrhea. Amenorrhea (cessation of menstruation) is frequently reported as a result of prolonged dieting.

Which Comes First, the
Depression or the Eating
Disorder?

A number of writers feel that depression is a cause not a result of bulimia (e.g., Pope & Hudson, 1984). While admitting that the question of cause and effect is still open, we are most impressed with studies such of those done by Russell (1979) and Fairburn (1985). Russell and Fairburn concluded from their studies that few clients with bulimia escape symptoms of depression but they feel the evidence is that these symptoms contribute to the perpetuation of the pattern of distress that these clients experience and do not cause bulimia. Russell (1979) noted that antidepressants or electro-convulsive therapy was effective in relieving the depressive symptoms in seven patients, but in no case was any change reported in the urge to overeat or to induce vomiting. Because the relief provided by antidepressant medication tended to be confined to the depressive symptoms, he felt that probably bulimia was not caused by a primary depressive illness. Fairburn (1985) took a different approach to answering this question. He found that careful history taking indicated that the depressive symptoms followed the start of the eating disorder. He further observed that once the eating disorder was under control that the depressive mood lifted. Fairburn felt that a minority of these clients had a primary affective disorder.

Have Studies Other Than Personality Tests Shown Behavioral Abnormalities?

While depression and irritability are routinely reported as emotional concomitants to dieting, other writers have reported other symptoms which are similar to those found in the studies using the MMPI reported earlier. Crisp (1981-82), among others, has pointed to the women's low self-esteem and fear of loss of control over their appetite and body weight. Crisp also stressed their joyless, impulsive sexual activity in fantasy or in reality. Beaumont, George, and Smart (1976) found histrionic personality traits in half of their clients and reported that obsessional traits also are common. Some writers (e.g., Garfinkel et al., 1980) are aware of acting out behavior such as the use of alcohol and street drugs. They also reported that individuals with bulimia were more likely to steal (probably as a way of supporting their binges). Also common to the group with bulimia were more frequent suicide attempts and acts of self-inflicted injury. The work by Garfinkel et al. (1980) is in agreement with the main premise of this chapter that individuals with bulimia, partly because of their constitutional tendency toward overweight and partly because of their personality, deal with their drive to be thin in an extreme fashion with phases of starvation giving way to bouts of binging.

What this points to is the complicated interaction between cause and effect. In the beginning, women with bulimia tend to have some personality characteristics in common (perfectionism, need for control, and so forth) which lead them to accept a program of strict dieting as a solution to their perceived lack of physical perfection. The strict dieting eventually leads to feelings of depression and other emotional reactions which interact with the pre-existant personality characteristics to create a reaction pattern (such as thoughts or attempts at suicide) which is beyond that found in the subjects in the semi-starvation study (Keys et al., 1985).

Earlier, we mentioned the impossible task society has set for women in terms of the model of thinness that is held as ideal. We now conclude that the seeds of defeat of attempts by women to lose weight and keep it off by normal methods exist from the beginning. What defeats them are their strong demands upon themselves to achieve a goal, and the natural biological consequences of attempting to adhere to a strict diet.

TRIGGERS FOR BINGING

Is Weight Control
Self-control?

In a previous chapter, we discussed how the presentation of the "ideal" woman in the media has evolved to a point where those women held up as beautiful are often very thin. This image is in conflict with the reality of the gradual increase in weight which has taken place in the population at large. We have spoken of the intense pressures this unrealistic ideal is placing on some women to diet and the adverse physical and emotional effects which are the result of this dieting. Bruch (1978) referred to this as a *"Sociocultural epidemic."* She indicated that this unrealistic ideal may affect vulnerable adolescents who come to believe that weight control is equal to self control and, if they can achieve weight control, they will be successful and beautiful. Later in the book, under our section on treatment, we will discuss this concept at more length as a problem that arises in therapy because of this "Magical Thinking."

Do Women Weighing Near
Their Set-point Regulate
Calorie Intake Better?

Normal weight subjects, that is, those individuals who are functioning within a limited range of weight around their set-point, show a good ability to regulate their calorie intake. These people do not show a tendency to suddenly eat large quantities of rich food. Those persons of all weights who are dieting and are functioning below their set-points will overeat under a number of conditions. Herman and Polivy (1975) found that nondieters lose weight when depressed but dieters gain weight—a point to be kept in mind. This suggests that food takes on a different meaning to deprived individuals, and that emotional distress acts to disrupt the inhibition of food intake to which the dieter precariously adheres.

What Is the Typical Pattern Leading to Bulimia?

When we look back at the histories of women who have bulimia, a pattern appears which has a number of steps. These steps are as follows:

1. the individual decides because of a life event such as rejection or teasing, to remake herself into a more perfect form by dieting,

2. the client then makes herself hungry over a period of time by keeping to a restrictive diet,

3. she begins to show an increased responsiveness to external food cues, especially sweet foods,

4. she becomes depressed and emotionally labile, and

5. this changes her ability to control the amount of food eaten and she must work harder to keep her behavior restrained in the presence of food.

The longer a woman maintains a diet and continues to stay below her natural weight, the more delicate the balance becomes and the more likely that something will occur which triggers a response breaking down her system of restraints. One of the factors leading to a lowered ability to continue eating with restraint is the emotional state which seems to be a natural consequence of semi-starvation. As we pointed out in the first half of this chapter, the emotional consequences of chronic dieting have been well substantiated and include irritability, poor concentration, anxiety, depression, apathy, lability of mood, fatigue, and social isolation (Keys et al., 1950; Bruch, 1973). The following sequence seems probable;

the long term food deprivation leads to the emotional responses that we have just given. These emotional responses in turn make for difficulty in maintaining the high level of restraint needed to remain on what is for that individual a semi-starvation diet. We would conclude that the process the woman has gone through to maintain her weight below it's normal set-point has become one of the factors which helped create her bulimia. This breakdown in restraint due to emotional responses which result from chronic hunger is compounded by the fact that food is something to which people often turn for consolation when they are unhappy. Many people who binge describe doing so either when they are alone and feeling miserable or as a way to avoiding doing something about problems. One of our clients upon reading this added, "and when I'm happy or the mailman comes or on Elizabeth's birthday."

A variety of reports (e.g., Hamburger, 1951) cite emotional stress as the trigger for overeating. When persons are under stress, eating only a small amount of some forbidden food is sufficient to break their restraint and cause them to binge uncontrollably. In a study by Pyle et al. (1981), patients were asked to select from a checklist possible feelings or thoughts associated with binge eating and asked to add any additional feelings or thoughts which they experienced prior to this behavior. Craving a certain food, having an uncontrollable appetite, and being unhappy seemed to precede the binges. Most individuals reported feeling guilty, worried, and full after an episode of binge eating.

Is the Restraint-Binge-Purge Cycle Repetitive?

The sequence begins with a long period of undernourishment, resulting in both an over responsiveness to food cues and a labile emotional state. When this state is coupled with even a minor outside stressor, the individual may seek to comfort herself by eating. This slip is sufficient to break through the restraints, resulting in an eating binge. This makes the person feel guilty for having failed, and she often responds by putting herself under an even tighter set of dietary restraints. This increased restraint produces the probability of even more binges and the pattern becomes established: restraint, binge, purge, restraint, and so forth.

TASTE AND HUNGER

As we continue to look more deeply into the phenomena called bulimia, we find that once an individual has developed the eating disorder, the condition creates factors which become self-perpetuating. In the previous section, we discussed how emotional stress triggers binges and how semi-starvation contributes to the emotional distress that provides the trigger. We also have seen how the body reacts to food deprivation by making the metabolism more efficient so that less food is needed to maintain a specific weight. This now brings us to the problem of taste and hunger.

Is Our Taste for
Food Determined
by Food Deprivation?

The reader will remember that we have been emphasizing the progression of symptoms which seem to occur in persons with bulimia. First is the strict dieting which may continue for some time; second is the development of an uncontrollable urge to gorge. As a reaction to this gorging, the woman then develops a pattern of fasting and/or purging. Evidence exists to show that a person's taste for certain kinds of foods is changed by the state of food deprivation.

What Kinds of Foods
Are Generally Eaten
During Binging?

Dally and Gomez (cited in Wardle & Beinart, 1981) discussed the differences in foods which are eaten during the dieting and the binging phases. In the diet phases, the woman eats the least palatable food, usually foods which are nonsweet. During a binge, however, the foods are usually sweet and/or highly palatable.

Along this line, Nisbett (1972) cited evidence that both deprived animals and humans are highly taste responsive and consume proportionally more good-tasting food as compared to what they would have eaten had they remained at a normal (for them) body weight. This desire to eat sweet food increases in relationship to the level of food deprivation which exists. These findings are similar to those of Hamburger (1951), who in a study of obese patients found that those who went on binges consumed large quantities of food with an emphasis on very sweet things. This behavior is very much like that of women with bulimia.

To understand how this increased urge to eat highly palatable food may work against the eventual goal of normal weight, we need to go back and look at Sclafanai and Springer's (1976) supermarket diet. The diet consisted of chocolate chip cookies, salami, cheese, bananas, marshmallows, mild chocolate, peanut butter, sweetened condensed milk, and a fat ration. The animals on this diet gained 269% more weight than did the controls who were fed a more regular diet during a two-month experiment. The effect of this rich diet was rapid and happened in a species which usually remained lean in the presence of abundant food.

What we have is a sequence in which hunger changes an individual's tastes so that sweetened or good tasting foods are preferred or craved. These are the foods that, when eaten in large amounts, are most likely to cause rapid weight gain and possibly, in some persons, an increase in the number of their fat cells. This increase in fat cells will cause more difficulty for them in losing and keeping off weight. Therefore what the individual is doing to fight off what she sees as excess weight is, in all probability, creating a situation in which she is much more likely to have a weight problem.

CHAPTER **6**

PERSONALITY
DYNAMICS

The factors that will predispose an individual to develop bulimia are present early in the individual's life. We find numerous commonalities in the family patterns of women with bulimia. While not all women with bulimia share all the features we will discuss, the family structure, goals, and interaction patterns do tend to be similar.

Case of Ruth

Ruth's family is typical of those reported by women with bulimia. She was the second child of four, with an older brother, a younger sister, and a younger brother. Her father was a civil engineer and her mother was a homemaker. From the time she was little she remembers that the assumption was that she would go to college. Her brothers were both involved in athletic competition, and Ruth competed on the swim team. Strong competition existed, especially between her and her older brother, to excel in school work.

Ruth's mother seemed often to be overwhelmed at managing her large family. She frequently confided in Ruth about her concerns about the other children and her husband. Ruth remembers helping her mother balance the checkbook each month and worrying whether or not they would have enough money. She was often placed in the position of having to ask her father to give her mother more household money with which to buy food. Because of her knowledge of the budget, Ruth developed a pattern of not asking for anything that cost money. She never wanted to cause her mother any further concern over finances.

As she was growing up, Ruth remembers her mother fighting a constant battle with weight. Her mother always seemed to be dieting. At one point, when Ruth was in therapy for bulimia, her mother confided that she had once been very underweight and had abused laxatives. Ruth's father also was weight conscious. Due to a childhood bout with polio, he had to walk with the aid of crutches. Gaining weight made maneuvering his crutches difficult for him.

What Are Common Family Characteristics?

Ruth's family illustrates several factors that we commonly find in the families of women with bulimia. The families are frequently intact with larger than average number of children. The fathers are usually professional men: engineers, physicians, businessmen, and so on. They are highly involved in their careers and may leave much of the child rearing to the mother. The mothers most often are homemakers, at least for the period when the children are at home.

Parents often expect high levels of achievement from the children which frequently results in competition between siblings. For example, Ruth recalled not feeling very close to her older brother and, at times, resenting him intensely because of his accomplishments. Many women with bulimia continue this pattern of intense competition into their adult lives, striving for high achievements, professionally, athletically, and in appearance. Although they often do very well, much of what they do accomplish gives them little satisfaction or the satisfaction is only temporary. Very few, if any, positive feelings about the achievement come from within these individuals. Their self-worth as persons seem to exist only as long as they have external validation. Although Ruth achieved very high grades in college, she was never content. Even those semesters when she had earned a perfect grade point average, she made comments about how she could have done better.

The family stress on achievement does have a positive side. The children in these families often do perform well. A common occurence is for a woman with bulimia to describe her siblings as, "My brother is at Harvard, my sister is getting her Ph.D. in agronomy, and my little brother just won a full scholarship." The child who develops bulimia often feels that she can never live up to the family standards, that she is inadequate by comparison to her siblings. Though she may feel hopeless, she still has an exceptionally high need to achieve.

Frequently a history of alcoholism or depression in other family members can be found. In Ruth's family, her younger sister had serious alcohol problems by the time she was twenty, and one of her uncles was an alcoholic.

Mothers of women with bulimia have often had difficulty maintaining their weight at their desired level. They are frequently on diets and are conscious of the calorie content of foods. As Ruth stated, "If I ever stop purging, I know exactly what I would look like. All the women on my mother's side of the family have the same body shape, small arms and legs and a thick middle."

**What Role Does the Child
with Bulimia Play in the
Family?**

Several themes repeat in the stories these young women tell of their families. Because the woman often feels that she can't compete successfully in the family as the "brain" or the "athlete," she may assume the role of the *responsible child* in the family. She will often take on many of the responsibilities generally considered parental activities. This responsibility may be the only way she sees to get the praise and approval for which she is so hungry. The responsible child is the child on whom everyone knows they can count to be reliable. Sometimes the role is developed in contrast to a family member who is troubled. In these families a good child/bad child comparison is set up. In either situation, the child is maintaining a role that is a strain. She constantly has the feeling that she is pretending to be something other than what she really is. "My parents think I am so perfect. They don't think I have any problems. If they ever found out what I do, they would freak out."

In families where one of the parents is unable or unwilling to perform as a parent, a blurring of the family boundaries may occur. One of the children, often the oldest female child, assumes the role of the responsible child very early in life and takes over the care of the house and/or younger siblings at a young age. In this situation, the individual feels great responsibility but also realizes she has little real control. In Ruth's case, we see this in the responsibility she felt in balancing the checkbook with her mother because "We all knew Mom was hopeless at math." Mom also confided in her, sharing too many of her worries. "There never seemed to be enough money at the end of the month. While we never actually ran out of food, I remember frequently worrying that there wouldn't be anything to eat." Ruth spent a lot of time as a child, worrying about things over which she had no control.

Case of Wendy

> *Another client described her situation: "I was the oldest of nine children. My mother never seemed to have time for us. I guess she was always having another baby. My father had a violent temper and physically abused us. I took over raising the other kids, especially the little ones. When my father got mad, I tried to distract his attention from the one he was mad at. Frequently, I took the abuse or we both did. One time my father beat my little brother and threw him outside wearing only his pajamas. It was snowing. He wouldn't let him in and wouldn't let me go to him. All I could do was look out the window and cry and hope he would see that I cared about him."*

For some of the women, the role of the responsible child was taken on when a parent became disable or died. "My mother developed epilepsy when I was twelve. I took over managing the home and she became an invalid." Another client stated, "When my father died the minister and family friends said that I needed to be a grown-up and help Mom take care of my brother."

Often the responsibility of being a parent figure to a younger sibling leaves the older child feeling helpless and inadequate. "My thirteen year old sister comes to me asking for help with things she can't tell my mother. Last month, she thought she might be pregnant and I know she is into drugs. I don't know what to do to help her but I know I can't tell my parents. My father would kill her."

Is the Girl with Bulimia Often the "Good Child?"

Another role the child may take on is that of the "good" child. This role is different from that of the responsible child in that it does not include the taking on of parental responsibilities. One of the real difficulties of being the good child in a family is that she feels she must never have any problems or complaints. The family system is already overloaded with problems and she feels guilty whenever she has to ask for anything. Part of her value as a person becomes connected to her not needing to ask for anything. This may be reinforced by the parents who make comments like, "Susan, you are so good. I always know we can count on you. I don't know how we would manage if you got into trouble like your sister."

If one of the children in the family is acting out, the *"good child/bad child"* dichotomy may develop. This is a situation where one child attempts to compensate for the trouble being caused by the other by being as perfect as possible. In our experience, when a "good child/bad child" dichotomy occurs, the child with bulimia is always in the "good child" position. "My sister caused my parents so much heartache, I couldn't bear to hurt them. She is taking drugs and staying out all night. She has run away from home twice." The "good child" develops a pattern of anticipating the desires of the parents and attempting to fill them. The parents are often relieved to have such a model child because of the turmoil created by the "bad child." The parents frequently respond by treating their model daughter as older than she really is.

Sometimes the "good child" role comes into being after one of the parents develops a problem. "My father lost his job two years ago and has been driving a bus since then. His drinking really picked up when he was laid off, and he started staying out all night. My mother is basically supporting the family with her secretarial job, but money is really tight. They fight a lot and Mom comes to me to talk when she is upset. Mom accidentally got pregnant with Bobby just as Dad lost his job. If it wasn't for Bobby, I think they would be divorced now. I try to take care of him and keep out of everybody's way. I really feel guilty about all the food I waste, especially with money so tight, but I can't help it."

In Childhood Did She Receive the Nuturing She Wanted?

Despite the pride that is felt for not needing anything, something is missing. Frequently a feeling is present of not being nurtured or taken care of in the way she feels she needs to be. For example, Ruth recalls an instance where her sister had been given a large birthday party but when her birthday came around she heard her parents discussing it, "We really can't afford to have a party for Ruth. She can manage better than Kathy. I know she will understand if we explain it to her."

Another client expressed the feelings that, "I never really felt like my parents were looking out for me. I was afraid a lot but I always acted like I knew exactly what I was doing. I used to fantasize that I was like the poor little match girl, standing outside the window in snow watching the entire family. There was such a feeling of longing to be taken care of."

In summary, one can find often a blurring of the boundaries in families of women with bulimia. Parents may not be functioning in appropriate parental roles. One of the parents may be acting as a dependent or irresponsible child. The child who goes on to develop bulimia may become a parent figure to the younger siblings and take over adult responsibilities in the home. She may become a confidant to the mother and take on worries about the well-being of the family that are inappropriate for her age. The end result is a child who is acting much older than her real years, feels guilty if she has to ask for anything, and at the same time, feels a real longing to be nurtured and taken care of.

PERSONAL DYNAMICS

Certain personality features tend to be common among women with bulimia. Not all of the women will possess all of these traits, however, most will exhibit several of these features. We have already mentioned the high needs for achievement and the perfectionism that develop in the woman from interactions with her family. In this section we will go on to explore other personality features that are common in women with bulimia, such as (1) a strong need for control, (2) cognitive rigidity, (3) polarity thinking, (4) difficulty dealing with men, and (5) an intense dislike for her body.

What Is their Need
for Control Like?

Being in control of their lives is important to women with bulimia. While this is true for many people, the areas they choose to control lead to further problems. One of these areas of control is eating. Once the woman has decided to lose weight, she goes on a strict, highly controlled diet. Often a constant battle emerges against the urge to eat. To maintain control, the woman may structure her day to allow almost no opportunity to eat. One college student had every minute of her day planned with classes, study periods, and exercise in a deliberate attempt to avoid being able to eat. This, of course, left her ravenous at the end of the day, which resulted in total loss of control and binge eating. The loss of control fueled the fear that, if given the slightest chance, she would eat constantly and become obese. Therefore, she would make a vow to be in even tighter control of her eating the next day.

Sometimes the need to be in control expresses itself in other situations besides those connected with food. One woman, who was employed as a secretary, never wanted to admit to her bosses that she couldn't keep up with the work she was asked to do. As she became more and more overloaded, she stopped taking breaks, took no lunch hour, and began working overtime without pay. For her to admit that she could not meet her expectations to perform to perfection was impossible, so instead she was overwhelmed with the job. She was aware that some of the other secretaries did considerably less work than she. In fact, although she would sometimes note that they were reading a book as she was struggling to keep up, she would never complain or ask for help. She ended up leaving her well paying job, rather than give up the illusion she had created that she was in total control of the situation.

This fear of loss of control followed by intensified efforts to maintain control can lead to feeling under constant stress. This leads to the development of an increasingly rigid lifestyle. One client illustrated the stress caused by this constant effort when she said, "Sometimes I want to strangle myself, I want to be in control so bad. When I fight the hardest for control is when it is the worst."

Do Clients with Bulimia
Hold to a "Right Way" to
Do Things?

The perfectionism and need for control results in a type of thinking, a *cognitive rigidity,* that is characteristic of women with bulimia. This is expressed in the conviction that there is a "right" way to do things and all other ways are considered "wrong." This rigidity becomes a part of the problem. For instance, in her attempt to control the binging, one woman ate at precisely the same time each day and ate exactly the same foods at each meal. If she varied from this routine for any reason, she had "failed" and a binge resulted. For example, her feeling was, "If I eat even one cookie, I have blown it and I might as well eat the entire box. Lots of times I don't stop there, I clean out the entire refrigerator." This type of behavior was also commented on in the studies on dieters who restrained themselves to the point of intense hunger. If they were given a small "preload" such as a cookie, the restraints broke down and excessive eating took place. The rigid structure this client imposed on her eating behavior also prevented her from partaking in any social activities that involved eating or took place over a meal time.

Another woman approached studying in the same rigid way. She planned on many hours of study time each night and felt guilty if anything interfered with her plan. If, for some reason, she was prevented from spending the allotted time on her school work, a substantially increased effort was vowed for the next night.

Do These Clients Think
in Terms of Good and Bad?

One result of cognitive rigidity is *"polarity thinking."* On the continuum of possible behaviors for any given situation, the entire middle of the continuum has been deleted, leaving only the extreme positive and negative values. For example, "good" food and "bad" food both exist. Good food is usually low in calories and is nutritious. Frequently, the woman will be vegetarian, focusing on organically grown products and excluding items such as refined sugar and processed grain products. Bad food is the food on which they binge. This usually includes high carbohydrate, high calorie foods such as doughnuts, candy bars, sweetened cereal, potato chips, and ice cream. In addition to thinking of food in this fashion, the label extends to the individual. "When I am eating 'good' food, I am good; when I eat 'bad' food, I am bad." This good/bad polarity is applied to other areas too. "If I get an 'A' on my test, I am good. If I run every day, I am good." If performance is less than the stated goal of perfection, the client feels out of control and the opposite polarity is felt, "I am bad." One client expressed the feeling that, "If I give up the 'bad' girl, I can't have any fun. If I give up the 'good' girl, I won't be loved."

Do Women with Bulimia Have
Difficulty Dealing with Men?

Yes, many women with bulimia do have difficulty dealing with *men*. They are very sensitive to rejection and have high needs for approval. They often do not view themselves as loveable, after all, they fall so far short of their own standards of perfection. They may have real reservations about having another person know what their body looks like. Because of the fear of rejection, the woman may avoid long term involvements with men. "I have a bad case of second date syndrome. After the second date, I find so many faults with him that I don't go out with him again." Women with bulimia seem to vacillate between a strong need to be taken care of and a fear of being taken advantage of. One woman stated that she had two categories of men, those who are rescuers and those needing to be rescued. She had difficulty relating to men who were not in either of these categories.

Another woman expressed her conflicts about relating to men: "If they like me as a person, I am afraid. I feel so unlovable. Maybe they could give me the love I need but I am afraid to accept it. I can't trust because I am sure I am unlovable. Part of me is starting to feel OK, but it's still a small part."

A major decision is whether to tell a man about the eating behavior or not. They fear rejection as if it were virtually inevitable. Their logic seems to be "If my boyfriend finds out about the bulimia, he will think I am disgusting, however, if I quit binging and purging, I will become obese and he will reject me because of that."

A woman who has been married for several years often will report that her husband does not know about her binge-purge habit. When he learns about the bulimic behavior, the man is surprised and puzzled, but this knowledge does not usually mean the end of the relationship. Indeed, for the woman involved, the guilt of keeping the secret has been so difficult to bear and the anticipation of rejection has been so strong, that a profound feeling of relief emerges once the secret is shared.

Do Women with Bulimia
Dislike Their Bodies?

In her book, *Femininity,* Susan Brownmiller asked the questions: "At what age does a girl child begin to review her assets and count her deficient parts? When does she close the bedroom door and begin to gaze privately into the mirror at contortionist angles to get a view from the rear, the left profile, the right, to check the curve of her calf muscle, the shape of her thighs, to ponder her shoulder blades and wonder if she is going to have a waistline? And pull in her stomach, throw out her chest and pose again in search for the most flattering angle, making a mental note of what needs to be worked on, what had better develop, stay contained, or else? At what age does the process begin, this obsessive concentration on the minutiae of her physical being that will occupy some portion of her waking hours quite possibly for the rest of her life?" (Brownmiller, 1985, p. 25)

This criticism of the body is common among women but is carried to the extreme by women with bulimia. Their criticism, their dislike for their bodies, is often intense and may amount to virtual rejection of their physical self. Women may reject aspects of their bodies for a variety of reasons. The reasons we will discuss revolve primarily around having been different from others because of something about their body such as (1) childhood obesity, (2) being unusually tall as a child, (3) having a chronic medical problem that made them different from other children, or (4) childhood physical or sexual abuse.

Is Childhood Obesity a
Common Characteristic?

Our observations support those found by other researchers that the history of women with bulimia often includes being overweight as children. Siblings and other children often can be incredibly cruel to overweight children damaging their self-image and self-respect. Lynn recalled, "When I was a kid, I can remember when my cousins played basketball, I had games of 'pig' dedicated to me." Pat remembers, "I can remember from the first grade on being tormented by boys. Nobody had to tell me I was fat in my family, because my sister was a year and a half older and was skinny. It was obvious that I was fatter. She got lots of attention and coaxing to eat."

Sometimes the relationship with the parents seems altered by being overweight. Ruth had been underweight and somewhat sickly as a little child. She had been encouraged to "eat so you can be big and strong." Being a very good little girl, Ruth did eat. In fact, she did very well and became overweight. She then was told, "Don't eat. You don't need that, you are too heavy." Ruth has unhappy memories of her father taking food off her plate in an effort to control her eating. She said, "I remember being taken to the ice cream store and I only got one scoop because I was too fat and the other kids got double dips. Dad also ate the chocolate rabbit out of my Easter basket but never any one else's. I grew up hating my body because 'it' did this to me." When asked what "it" did, Ruth replied, "I guess I felt that my parents didn't love me as much as the other kids. I know this isn't true, but it felt that way."

An interesting event is to have the client bring in a picture of herself at the age when she was teased about her weight. What you usually see in the picture is a somewhat plump little girl but not one who is as grossly obese as the client has been describing herself.

Can Being a Tall
Child Be a Problem?

Occasionally, the feeling of being different comes from having been exceptionally tall, especially if the height occurs at an early age. Sherry stated, "I was the tallest kid in the sixth grade. By the time I was eleven, I was already 5'7". My brothers' nicknames for me were Moose and Truckie. When I was on the swim team, my teammates picked it up and you could hear them yell 'come on Truckie!' when I was swimming. That was one of the reasons I quit the team."

Gina was also tall and somewhat overweight when she was young. "I remember when I was in grade school. Each year we would all have to line up, boys and girls together, while the school nurse measured our height and weight. She would call out the numbers to someone else who was writing it down. I could feel the conversation die down as I approached the scales. When the nurse called out the numbers, 'five feet eight inches, one sixty three,' I could hear the buzzing start. I wished I could have dropped through the floor.''

Have Many Women with Bulimia Had a Chronic Medical Problem Which Made Them Different Than Other Children?

Sometimes the issue is not weight or height that makes women with bulimia reject their bodies, but medical problems they may have. The diabetic patient with bulimia presents special problems to her physician (Hillard & Hillard, 1984). Because of the dietary restrictions and insulin injections, the diabetic patient may come to view her body as deficient and feel that her body is preventing or cheating her from living a normal life. She may experiment with increasing the amount of insulin she gives herself in an attempt to burn extra calories. Binging on carbohydrates can be especially dangerous for these clients.

One woman with whom we worked had very negative feelings toward her body because she had Turner's syndrome. Because of this problem, Laurie's body did not go through puberty at the appropriate time. When she was sixteen and had not begun physically developing, her parents took her to a physician who diagnosed the disorder and placed her on hormone therapy so that her body would go through puberty. She also learned that because of the Turner's syndrome, she would never be able to bear children. Laurie expressed the feeling that ''my body is one of God's rejects.'' She had considerable doubts about her ability to attract a husband because she could not have children.

Celiac disease is a disorder that causes a person to be unable to tolerate grain products. Linda had a pattern of binge eating for years. She did not use laxatives but had found that eating a ''box of shredded wheat'' would be followed by massive diarrhea. After the grain intolerance was diagnosed, she actively resented the dietary limitations she was forced to follow. She also maintained an image of her ideal weight as what she had weighed when her illness caused her body to drop well below a healthy weight for her height.

What Influence Might Childhood Abuse Have on These Clients?

Some of the women describe discipline that was very severe in their families. Often, they do not think of the discipline as having been unusual. Sharon described "belt-whippings" that she received at least once a week. She remembers one entire summer that she couldn't go swimming because she didn't want anyone to see the bruises down the backs of her legs. When the therapist referred to this as child abuse, she was astonished. "I always thought that was the way it was for everyone."

When a history of sexual abuse is present, then women often express the feeling that their bodies are "dirty" or "damaged goods." Gina had been raped by her grandfather after several years of incidences of inappropriate touching. She described her reaction. "For a long time I felt my body wasn't real. I had this mental image of a tall, buxom blonde and my body wasn't it. After the rape, I used to believe I could separate from my body and then if he did things to me, he was only doing it to my body, not me." At one time she spoke of being outside her body and at another time, of going inside to a small dark place where no one else could ever get.

Mary had been molested by her father for years. She described feeling like her body was "dirty or damaged goods." She was considerably overweight and had an awareness that being fat protected her from men seeing her as a sexual being. "Getting fat was one way I could get back at my father. He did not find me attractive when I was overweight." Mary had gone on to college and had gotten married. She stated that she had fairly normal sexual interaction with her husband. She initially described that she had a strong negative response to being touched by her husband in ways that reminded her of her father touching her. These aversions subsided as angry feelings toward her father and mother were explored in therapy.

Regardless of how these feelings developed of having a body that is different, deviant, or rejectable, they remain with the women as they become adults. "When I walk across campus and hear guys laugh, it's that same laughter and the feelings come back. Though I tell myself it's not true, I know they are laughing at me."

The extent of the rejection of the physical self was expressed by Gina. "I sometimes wish I could leave my body behind and go on without it. Just leave it sitting there in a chair and find some other body to be in."

This separation of the mental and physical self also is expressed by the feeling that the two parts are virtually at war with each other. If the body has its way, the fear is that she will become obese. "I only feel good when my mind is winning and my body is getting thinner and thinner. Even then, I feel that I must be constantly vigilant." What seems to happen is that periods of "mind control" emerge when binging occurs. This warfare leaves the individual in a constant state of turmoil.

The designation of the body as the "enemy" makes some of the self-destructive behavior characteristic of bulimia more understandable. The fact that vomiting and laxative use are painful and potentially damaging to the body does not have the same effect on women with bulimia as it would on someone who values their body. This also explains why exercise can be tolerated beyond the point of pain. Some other women refuse to even consider exercise as a potential tension reliever. "I never do anything for my body like exercise. I see others doing it and know I would feel better, but I won't let myself."

CHAPTER 7

EARLY STAGES
OF TREATMENT

Most women with bulimia view their behavior as undesirable and would like to be able to stop. At the same time, they are terribly afraid of giving it up. They frequently have few, if any, other coping skills for dealing with stress, anger, or their intense fear of becoming fat. Although they often have not lost much weight through purging, they develop a strong belief that, if they were ever to stop, they would gain to the point of obesity. The therapist must be aware of the client's ambivalence about changing her eating behavior and not try to move to eliminate immediately the bulimic behavior. A helpful idea may be to regard the binge eating as a symptom resulting from a constellation of situational, personality, and family factors. Approaching the eating symptom directly is almost certainly destined for failure and will damage the therapist's credibility with the client. Most of the women with bulimia have attempted to stop the binge-purge cycle many times. Indeed, a common happening is for the woman to promise herself, after each episode of binging and purging, to never do it again. If the therapist attempts to alter the eating pattern, those attempts probably will duplicate things she has already tried and will only reinforce the feelings of helplessness and failure that already exist.

What Are Some Expectations in the Initial Phase of Therapy?

The initial phase of therapy begins when the individual realizes she has come into contact with someone who is knowledgeable about bulimia. With many of these clients several previous attempts have been made to get help from professionals; however, these experiences often have been negative. Physicians and mental health professionals who do not have experience or knowledge of eating disorders may be incredulous or judgmental when told of the eating behavior. Frequently the woman has been told "Just stop it! All you need is will power."

One can see how women with bulimia are reluctant to reveal their problem to a therapist. They may "try out" a therapist for several sessions on another problem before disclosing the eating disorder. To be effective the therapist must respond in an empathetic, nonjudgmental fashion to the information when it is offered. A crucial point to remember is that the client anticipates rejection for what she regards as "disgusting" behavior. The therapist's accepting attitude is often the first step in the individual realizing "maybe I'm not so crazy after all." Also helpful is for her to realize that the therapist has heard of the problem before. Despite frequent articles in popular magazines and newspapers, the client still may maintain the feeling that she is the only person who has ever done this "deviant" behavior.

Another factor that may make the client even more hesitant to reveal her eating problem is if the therapist is a male. Many of these women have a very strong desire for approval from men and are especially sensitive to *any indication* of rejection. *The idea of "confessing" her behavior to a male who may disapprove, is highly negative.*

**When and How Is
the Bulimia Revealed?**

Some clients may come in seeking help with a problem that is a peripheral issue to the bulimia. Other problems such as depression, mood swings, difficulty with parents or roommates, money problems, and dating concerns are issues often related to the eating disorder. In some cases, the counselor may have to do some detective work to piece together the whole story. For example, one client had been asked twice by her therapist if anything was different or unusual about her eating habits. She denied having any problem in that area. As the sessions progressed and the pieces accumulated, the therapist finally said, "Amy, I just can't believe that you haven't had problems with your eating behavior." Her reply was, "Well, yes, I have had bulimia off and on for three years, but I hadn't binged or purged for two weeks when you asked me about my eating, so I said I had no problem." One of the ways a therapist can ask about potential eating problems is to say something like, "It wouldn't be unusual for someone with your history to also be having problems controlling her eating behavior. I'm wondering if you ever had trouble in this area?" By phrasing your comment this way, you are not only communicating that you know something about the area but you also are saying that you wouldn't be surprised by the revelation.

A complete description of the eating problem should be obtained from the client. This should be done both to know the extent of the problem and to form a baseline against which progress can be measured. The following six questions provide a checklist of things that need to be asked and about which information needs to be obtained.

1. *How often do you binge eat?* The therapist should be aware that the frequency of binge behavior is often underreported. Also a pattern may exist of binging followed by vomiting and then returning to eat more and purge again. This cycle may repeat several times but be reported as one binge by the client.

2. *What ways do you use to avoid retaining the calories you consume?* The variety or responses to this question are sometimes amazing. The most common are vomiting, laxative abuse, diuretics, exercise, and practicing a binge/fast cycle. If laxatives or diuretics are mentioned, be sure to ask how many are taken. One may find that the woman is using

far above the recommended dosage. Ask what kind and how much exercise the person is doing. The answer may indicate a devotion to exercise that is far above average, for instance, running 10 to 15 miles each day, or taking several aerobics classes a day, or a combination of several strenuous activities.

One nurse said she would never take laxatives to try to lose weight because they would be harmful to her health. Instead, she ate handfuls of sorbitol sweetened mints which gave her diarrhea. She always kept at least 5 packages in her purse at all times.

Another client reported that she would turn the shower on full blast with the hottest water. When the bathroom filled with steam, she would put on heavy clothes and her winter coat and do exercises in order to lose weight.

A variation of this method was described by another client. She would put on two layers of sweat suits before going to bed. She would then turn the electric blanket on high and go to sleep. She reported that she usually would be able to withstand it until three or four in the morning when she would wake up drenched with sweat.

Clients seem to pay little heed to the fact that laxatives, diuretics, and sweating do little except dehydrate the body. The water that is lost is quickly replaced as soon as fluids are consumed. The actual calorie loss from laxative overdose was measured by Bo-Lynn, Santa-Ana, Morawski, and Fordtran (1983). They found that a loss of *less than 200* calories occurred even when *50* laxatives were taken. This information will have little effect on the client. What seems to be important is the number on the scale, not how it is reached or how permanent it is.

3. *What has been your highest and lowest weight at your present height?* This will give the therapist an idea of the amount of fluctuation in the woman's weight. Commonly 20 or more pounds difference may be found between the highest and lowest weight, sometimes over a relatively short period of time.

4. *What is your present weight and height?* The answer for weight is often well within normal limits for the individual's height. The therapist should not bother to give reassurance that the client is not overweight. She does not consider this information relevant in any way.

5. *What do you see as your ideal weight?* This figure is often 10 to 20 pounds lower than is average for her height. The answer to the question will give the therapist an idea of just how unrealistic the client's expectations are of herself. The therapist should remember that sharing his/her opinion that the client's goal is unrealistic is not likely to be helpful and may cause the client to regard the therapist as not understanding the client's needs.

6. *Are you willing to be examined by a medical doctor for the purpose of assistance in treatment of your bulimia?* During or near the end of the first session, the therapist should recommend that the client see a physician for a general check-up and to check for physical damage from the bulimia. The therapist should have a physician in mind who is knowledgeable about eating disorders and is nonjudgmental in his/her approach. The client should sign a "release of information" form allowing the therapist to talk to the physician about her. The therapist probably will call the physician prior to the client's visit to let him/her know any medical areas about which the therapist is particularly concerned. Even if the client reassures the therapist that she sees her physician regularly, she should make an appointment anyway because she may have seen him/her for years without revealing her eating behavior.

EARLY SESSION ISSUES

In addition to the information gathered about the eating disorder, some other areas should be covered during early phases of client/therapist interaction. Mood swings, especially following binge/purge behavior are common. The therapist also needs to deal with the client's ambivalence, if any, about being in counseling with the intention of giving up her bulimic behavior. Reframing the behavior, prescribing the symptom, and removing the deadlines are all interventions that can help the client overcome the ambivalence.

Will Mood Swings Be Considered Early in Therapy?

One very important issue which needs to be discussed early is the client's mood swings. Feelings of depression are common in these clients, especially following a binge/purge episode. Other times when they are likely to feel depressed are after interaction with her family, after a breakup with a boyfriend, or after a "failure" such as getting a lower than expected grade on an exam. The therapist should ask specific questions about suicidal thoughts and possible past suicide attempts. If it is appropriate, the therapist should make a no-suicide contract with the client. One form to use is: "I promise not to hurt myself, accidentally or on purpose, without talking to you first." Emphasize that attempting to call the therapist is not sufficient. She must continue trying to reach the therapist until she contacts him/her even if it means delaying any action for several hours.

If the client appears to be quite depressed, an *immediate* referral to a physician may be appropriate. Sometimes, if the risk of suicide is high, anti-depressive medication and or hospitalization may be necessary.

How Do the Therapist and Physician Work Together?

The physician is a very important member of the treatment team. He/she takes responsibility to check out any physical complications resulting from the bulimic behavior. If anti-depressant medications are necessary, the physician will be the one to prescribe them.

The physician will ultimately be responsible for the decision to hospitalize the patient if she is suicidal, severely malnourished, or has medical complications that require inpatient management. Also helpful, in a team approach, will be to have the physician monitor the client's weight especially if she is progressively losing. The therapist will have difficulty being responsible for the client's emotional well-being and at the same time being in charge of her weight management.

Are Ambivalent Feelings
Natural During Therapy?

Yes, the therapist should be aware that by revealing the eating disorder, the client may find a considerable number of negative thoughts and feelings surfacing. As the negative thoughts and feelings come up, considerable anxiety may be produced. The client may well have second thoughts about returning for more counseling. To help ease this situation, the therapist might say something like "You may be feeling a little uncomfortable about having told someone about your eating problems. This is a very natural response. Part of you may even be thinking of not coming back, however, another part of you knows you can't do it by yourself and you really want to get help."

The therapist may find this ambivalence resurfacing periodically during the course of therapy. A resistance seems to exist to the idea of needing help, accompanied by an awareness that they really need the help.

Some Therapists Reframe
the Behavior. Why?

One way of reducing some of the guilt associated with the revelation of the eating behavior is to reframe it in a less malignant fashion. The type of statement the therapist might make is, "I view all human behavior as intended to help the individual. In the case of bulimia, the behavior is intended to reduce stress and anxiety. Unfortunately, it does its job very well or it would not be so difficult to give up. The price you pay, however, is negative feelings about yourself and potential serious damage to your body."

This reframing of the behavior as "intended to help" relieves some of the guilt and stress involved with the eating problem. By acknowledging how much difficulty she has in stopping the bulimic behavior, the therapist indicates both an understanding of the tenacity of the problem and gives the person credit for having tried to stop on her own. Most have tried many times to stop, in fact, many promise themselves each time they binge that they will never do it again. When they do repeat the behavior, they have "failed" and feel inadequate and guilty.

Why Do Therapists
Sometimes Prescribe Binging?

Prescribing the symptom as a treatment procedure always comes as a surprise to the client. The way to prescribe the symptom is to say something like "It will be important for you to continue the binging for a while so that we may more clearly understand what the bulimia is helping you to deal with. I want you to be sure, between now and when I see you next, to binge at least once. When you do, I want you to pay special attention to how you are feeling before you binge. What has happened leading up to the eating episode? What are you thinking about? What physical sensations in your body are you aware of?"

This treatment procedure is important for several reasons. First, it reduces the guilt when the client does binge, which is sure to happen. After all, her therapist told her to do so. Second, it relieves the anxiety that is often present that, "Now that I have seen someone for the problem, I will have to stop right away." The third benefit is that this step will give both the client and the therapist information on problems underlying the behavior. Becoming aware of the emotions preceding a binge often comes as a surprise to the client because they frequently are remarkably naive or denying of a relationship between feelings and behavior. They hold the illusion that the need to binge descends mysteriously over them and is irresistible.

How Long Does Therapy Take?

Removing the deadlines as to when the bulimia will change is essential. The client must realize that therapy for bulimia may take an extended time period. This is not short term therapy. The two, client and therapist, need to discuss this because often the client comes for counseling wanting a rapid cure. Remember, the client is a perfectionist with high need for approval. The therapist does not want the client pressuring herself to respond rapidly and to feel like she is disappointing the therapist at the same time. In some cases, the issue may necessitate informing boyfriends, husbands, or parents of the long term nature of the problem to avoid them pressuring the client. As therapists we usually speak in terms of therapy taking a year and often longer. The therapist will have to estimate the expected treatment time by considering the severity of the problem. The longer the person has had bulimia and the more times she binges daily, the longer the time needed to give it up. To overestimate the time is better than to underestimate it.

The client must also realize that the cessation of binges does not occur abruptly. To make this point, the therapist might say, "You may not know exactly when your last binge occurred. What usually happens is that they get further and further apart and less intense until they gradually fade out. They will stop when you have learned other coping skills and no longer need to binge."

Despite the therapist's best efforts to assure the client that the bulimia will not change immediately, discouragement is common in the early phases of counseling. This feeling was expressed by Sharon in a poem she wrote after being in counseling one month.

> I don't feel much better than I did last night,
> I'm tired of doing what's always so right.
> I've given all that I've got to give,
> I don't care anymore, I don't want to live.
> Why doesn't she let me die?
> Instead she made me promise I wouldn't try.
> I wonder, why doesn't she just give up.
> I can't handle this, I guess I'm not so tough.
> My friends and family think I've got it together so well
> What they don't know is what I'll never tell.
> She says, "Talk to me, I really do care."
> But sometimes I think, "Do I dare?"
> She asks, "When are you ever going to let someone in?"
> My reply to that is "Maybe I never can."
> She tells me to "hold on" that I can win,
> Well, I know I'm just existing 'til the end.

In Summary, What Are Some Therapy Procedures Used Early in Treatment?

The therapist must recognize that he/she is dealing with a client with the potential for strong mood swings that may include suicidal thoughts or intentions. Recognition and treatment for these mood swings will be considered early. Also the option of immediate physician involvement will be considered if the client appears severely depressed. The ambivalence about committing to therapy that is designed to remove such a well entrenched coping skill will be treated. Also the therapist will need to reframe the bulimic behavior so that it does not appear as deviant.

Probably the therapist will prescribe the symptom as a means to remove guilt and to gather information on the needs that are driving the behavior. Information will be shared with the client to let her know that therapy is a slow gradual change, but that working together, the therapist and the client can bring about a solution to the problem.

CHAPTER **8**

LATER ISSUES
IN
THERAPY

Women with bulimia have thinking patterns that are characterized by rigidity and unreasonable demands and fears. As the therapist leaves the initial sessions, where he/she was primarily concerned with history taking and the establishment of rapport, the major focus of therapy shifts to modifying the thinking of the client. Some of the issues to be confronted are the unreasonable needs the client has to be in control at all times, rigid self-expectations, magical thinking, and fear of fat. Many of the women will have unresolved family issues. These will be discussed further in the chapter on family therapy. Also necessary, as part of the client's recovery, is for her to develop coping skills for dealing with stress.

MODIFYING THE THINKING

How Is the Need
for Control Treated?

As we have stressed repeatedly, control is a major issue in eating disorders. Women with bulimia often feel on the brink of losing control and they develop very rigid behavior patterns in their attempts to maintain it. For example, they may schedule their day very tightly in order to avoid binging. After having binged, they may try to go for extended periods of time without eating at all. Hunger, and thus the drive to binge, increases as they fight to avoid eating. They express the feeling that, "If I eat even one bite, I will binge uncontrollably." Because they constantly worry about what others think of them and about someone discovering their bulimia, they often go to great lengths to avoid discovery. One way they do this is by going from one fast food restaurant to another rather than consuming a large amount of food at any one place. If they vomit after binging, they know which restrooms in the dormitory or sorority house are empty around mealtimes.

Using a metaphor to explain the concept of *giving up control to get control* can be helpful. The one we often use is, "If you were to have a handful of sand and grip it very tightly, you would lose most of it over the sides of your hand and through your fingers. If, instead, you held the sand gently in your palm, you would keep most of it. That is giving up control to get control."

The therapist needs to emphasize that the change in control is not the same as "losing control." Losing control is what is feared the most by women with bulimia. What the therapist is striving to achieve and what the client needs to do is to gradually let go of the intensity with which she attempts to control herself and her world. This sand metaphor can be used throughout therapy when the client exhibits rigid thinking and behavior. Just the phrase, "remember the handful of sand, you are hanging on too tightly," will cause the client to pause and re-evaluate the situation.

Can the Therapist Help
Overcome the Absolutes?

Often clients with bulimia get caught up in "shoulds," "musts," and "oughts." "I must exercise every day." "I should get an A on every test." "I ought to please everyone at all times." "I need to have everyone like me." At first it will be difficult for the client to relax these absolutes. Because she has etablished goals based on these irrational "shoulds" and "musts," she is bound to fall short of them. The therapist will need to help the client develop flexibility in her thinking about what she is capable of realistically achieving.

One way for the counselor to help the client restructure her thinking, is to repeat the phrase *"It doesn't have to be that way."* The client needs help in developing alternatives so as to recognize other possibilities and in so doing change the "shoulds" to the more flexible "It would be nice if..." and the "musts" to "I would like to..." This kind of cognitive restructuring is an important step in overcoming the symptoms of bulimia.

Many times, the therapist will recognize that the client's thinking style is one that deals with polarities. Such thinking will cause the client to consider responses on an issue, problem, or situation as if the entire middle of the continuum of responses has been dropped out. What is left is "perfect" or "good" on one end and "imperfect" or "bad" on the other. All performance that is not "perfect" is automatically "bad." One client, Cindi, made a sign for her desk in her office that said, "THERE IS A MIDDLE!!" She laughed that she had gotten several comments on it. "It was hanging there in between 'Save the Whales' and 'Vote ERA.' People couldn't figure it out, but it helped me to look at it several times a day. I could feel the intensity slow down every time I saw it."

What is Magical Thinking?

Magical thinking, another cognitive process, must be confronted. "As soon as I _____ , I will be able to give up the bulimia." The blank is filled in with different words by the client such as the following:

Lose 10 pounds
Finish high school (college)
Move away from home (out of the dorm)
Get a boyfriend
Get married
Get pregnant ("I will have to stop
  when someone else's life is at stake.")
Get into graduate school
Get a job

The possible "if onlys" are practically endless, but each individual has her own event in mind after which she will be "cured." Of course, this is also an example of the feeling clients have that an external event will end their problem. This is part of the way clients use to deny the internal, emotional roots of their behavior.

One way the therapist can help to reduce the power of magical thinking is to ask the client what goals she had set up in the past that already have been reached. Perhaps, at one time, she had felt that, "As soon as I move out of my parents' house, I will be able to stop binging." The therapist then can confront her with the fact that she is now living in her own apartment and is still binging. Women with bulimia find it unpleasant to hear that many women with eating disorders continue the behavior after graduating from college, getting married, and through pregnancies. The ones who overcome their bulimia do so by dealing with the underlying emotional forces driving the behavior. The therapist can and will assist the client in this area.

How Is the Fear of
Becoming Fat Treated?

Part of the reason the bulimia is so difficult to give up is that the woman has an intense fear that, if she stops removing the calories from her body, she will become enormously fat. She is likely to have a mental image of how she would look, as well as a scenario constructed in which she is the object of ridicule and rejection. If she has been overweight in the past, as many of these women have, the picture and memories may be fairly accurate reconstructions of former experiences.

To contest the rationality of this fear is futile. If the therapist does, the woman is likely to agree with him/her on a cognitive, intellectual level, but retain the fear, unchanged, on an emotional level. Honestly informing the woman that she may experience a small three to five pound weight gain upon the termination of the purging may be helpful in counseling. This gain occurs primarily because the woman has kept herself in a dehydrated state with the vomiting, laxatives, or diuretics. A rebound retention of fluids takes place in which the body maintains a higher level of water in an attempt to avoid dehydration (Bo-Lynn, Santa-Ana, Morawski & Fordtran, 1983). This rebound fluid retention is gradually lost as the individual stops the dehydrating activities.

The weight gain also may be due to the additional bulk in the intestines that will become less as the chronic constipation lessens. Although neither of these factors represent gain of body fat, the increased weight may be greeted with alarm. A good practice is to have the client agree to weigh herself no more than once a week. Try to agree on a weight range of around five pounds that is acceptable, rather than a precise figure. This will help prevent panic at slight weight fluctuations. Sometimes the client wishes to get rid of her scale entirely and have someone else monitor her weight just to guarantee that she does not gain large amounts of weight.

Initial discussions that include asking the client to take a more flexible attitude toward the gaining of weight will likely be met with adamant refusal to consider any weight higher than the current one. Actually, many of the women would probably like to weigh less. Generally, the therapist is wise to not push this issue too hard. If the client feels the counselor is encouraging her to gain weight, she may drop out of therapy. We have found that even those who are most adamant about maintaining or losing weight gradually modify their position and accept the modest gains that usually occur. This shift occurs as needs for acceptance and perfection are modified and confronted in therapy. When these needs are no longer felt as intensely, the need to have the "perfect body" also is not as intense.

Can the Therapist Help with Calories and Meal Planning?

Many women with bulimia have no idea as to what a normal amount of food is for a meal or the number of calories they may consume and still maintain their present body weight. Many grossly underestimate the amount of food they may eat and consider the cost of giving up purging to be constant hunger and deprivation. Many of them started down this road when they couldn't stand the hunger or the stringent diets they had attempted.

The therapist knows the kind of eating habits, calorie intake, and meal planning practiced by women with bulimia. To assist the client the therapist generally works with a clinical dietitian who becomes a member of the team of specialists (medical doctor, dietitian, and therapist) who assist the client. The therapist generally refers the client to a dietitian for information and guidance in meal planning and a realistic eating plan. As with the physician, the dietitian must be someone familiar with the issues and problems of someone with an eating disorder. The therapist will obtain a release of information from the client so that the therapist may discuss concerns and progress with the dietitian. Thus the team members work cooperatively to assist the client.

**Summary of Maladaptive
Cognitive Patterns Treated**

In summary, after the working relationship is established the focus of therapy turns to the maladaptive cognitive patterns characteristic of women with bulimia. The high need to feel in control at all times is addressed. The client's rigid thinking and unreasonable demands which she is placing on herself need to be examined and modified. The therapist encourages the client to develop a middle ground of acceptability rather than defining everything, including herself, as either "good" or "bad." Magical thinking is decreased as the client learns through therapy to take responsibility for her own behavior. Fear of becoming fat is virtually universal among women with bulimia and is considered and treated throughout the counseling interaction.

TEACHING COPING SKILLS

**What Are the
Rewards for Binging?**

For women who are bulimic, binge eating is a very effective method for dealing with stress. This is especially true if purging follows the binge. Women who practice binging and purging report that, prior to the onset of a binge, they are feeling anxious and on edge. Often something has happened that was upsetting, such as an argument with a boyfriend or parents, a grade that was lower than they expected, or feeling awkward in a social situation. During the binge, which may last 1 to 2 hours, they describe a period that is free of thinking about their problems. Nothing exists for them except the food. Following the binge, especially if vomiting occurs, they describe an emotional numbness. This is not the same as feeling calm or neutral but is more like being emotionally anesthetized. The client may have feelings of guilt and depression about having given in to binging, however, the anxiety is gone. The woman is often very tired at this time.

**What Are Major Goals
of Therapy and Why?**

One of the major goals of therapy must be to teach alternative coping skills for dealing with stress and anxiety. The client should realize that the habit strength of the eating behavior is very strong. The coping skills must be approached, initially, as additional skills rather than alternatives to replace the binges. This is necessary because if they are presented as alternatives, the woman may either avoid the new coping skills entirely or feel a strong sense of failure when she cannot substitute them for binging. Gradually, as these additional skills are practiced regularly, the need to binge will become weaker. Eventually, the tensions that lead to the buildup of the drive to binge will be resolved by other stress relievers. The coping skills that we have found to be most useful are thought stopping, relaxation training, keeping a journal, assertiveness training, exercise, and calling a friend. We feel exercise is so important for a number of purposes that we are devoting a separate chapter to it.

**How Is "Thought
Stopping" Taught?**

As we have already mentioned, women with bulimia have high self-expectations of perfection and achievement. When something occurs so that these goals are not reached, they often dwell excessively on their "inadequacies." This may involve replaying a scene in their mind over and over, pointing out how "stupid" or "inadequate" they looked. They often go on to remind themselves of other times when they felt similarly and then "catastrophize" about how they probably never will be able to do anything right for the rest of their lives. One can see how, from one incident, bad feelings and anxiety can escalate into major proportions.

The goal of thought stopping is to cut off this escalation and relieve the constant pressure.

Elaine describes her pattern, "When something doesn't go right, like if I ask a question in class and it seems like the professor or other students think it is a stupid question, I immediately start my 'Fuck-up tapes.' It is my father's voice telling me that I am nothing but a fuck-up. I've never been any good and I never will be. I'm nothing but a lazy slob. I never do anything right. I'm a total failure." This internal dialogue continues, building up the anxiety and guilt, until Elaine silences it with a binge and purge session. Sometimes binging and purging several times in rapid succession are necessary before being able to turn off the "Fuck-up tapes."

A suggested procedure for teaching thought stopping is for the therapist to present it in this fashion: "A lot of how you feel is determined by what you are thinking about. Negative thoughts lead to negative feelings. If you wanted to depress yourself right now, how would you do it?" The client generally doesn't have to think very long to come up with a topic to dwell upon that would lead to feeling negatively about herself. After doing so, the therapist can point out to her that she is probably feeling a little bad just having focused on that topic for a few minutes.

Then the therapist might say "Now, let's generate a few things that you can think about that are neutral." Looking for "neutral" thoughts seems to work better, that is, thoughts that don't have either a positive or negative connotation to them. Thinking "happy" thoughts has somewhat of a "Pollyanna" quality to it that makes them more difficult to substitute when an individual is already somewhat depressed or anxious. If the client has difficulty generating neutral topics, the therapist might suggest pets, favorite hobbies, television shows, movies, or books, things that the client has done or knows. The idea is to have something already in mind to substitute when the negative thoughts start. If a person is already in the negative cycle, generating a topic can be difficult, so having one ready to use can really help.

Next the therapist will say to the client something like "When you find yourself starting to put yourself down and to dwell on negative happenings, I want you to mentally shout 'STOP!' If you are alone, you can even shout it aloud. Visualize a large red STOP sign in your mind. Then deliberately turn your thoughts to one of the neutral topics you have just developed. This may seem simple, but it's not as easy as it sounds. It will get easier as you practice."

As with all new behavior, thought stopping feels awkward at first. For the client to practice a few times during the therapy session may help. The client will need to bring to mind a depressing thought, then use the word "STOP" and the mental picture of the STOP sign, and then introduce the neutral thoughts.

Relaxation training. At the same time the client is learning techniques to deal with self-deprecating and stress producing thoughts, a helpful approach would be to learn some methods of general stress reduction. One of the most helpful techniques is relaxation training. The book, *The Relaxation Response* (1976) by Benson with Klipper, is an excellent source of instructions that may be read and followed by the client. Many good pre-recorded tapes are available to teach relaxation, or the therapist may wish to make a tape which is personalized to the client's individual needs.

One of the ways the therapist may explain to the client the need for relaxation training is to say: "Your body is already conditioned to respond to a variety of stimuli with tension. Lower than expected grades, not looking your best, someone making a critical remark, are all things that cause tension to build. What are you going to do is to teach your body to relax at your command. You cannot be both tense and relaxed at the same time. This will give you much more choice and control."

The following relaxation script is especially well suited to clients with bulimia because it emphasizes that their own body is controlling the rate and depth of relaxation. The wording is similar to what the therapist would say and do to assist the client. These instructions may be placed on a tape by the therapist and given to the client to use between therapy sessions.

Relaxation Exercise. "Find a comfortable position and prepare to take a brief vacation from any cares or worries going on in your every day life. To start the process of relaxation, I want you to focus on several sensations. Notice the feel of your head resting on the back of the chair. Notice the light touch of the hair on your forehead. The air feels cool on your neck where your blouse is open. Notice the fabric of your blouse over your shoulders. (Continue on down the body mentioning sensations of hands on the arm rests, jewelry on wrists or fingers, pressure of body against chair, feeling of shoes on feet, and so forth.)

Now to let your body help you relax still further, I want you to spend a few minutes focusing on the "still point." That quiet time after you let your breath out and before you take your next breath in. A pause when your lungs and your chest muscles are at rest. Notice that each time your body pauses at the "still point" that you gradually become more and more relaxed. (The client is given a full minute of silence to focus on her breathing.)

Now I want you to take a mental trip around your body searching out any areas of tension or tightness. As you encounter the tension, I want you to allow the tension to flow out of your body with the air as you exhale so that your body's own natural breathing rhythms will help and guide you into deep relaxation. Starting with your head and face, notice any areas of tightness around your eyes, your jaws, across your forehead. Notice these areas become relaxed as you exhale the tightness out of your body. Just let the tension flow gently away with the air. Now let your mind travel down to your neck and shoulders. Notice any tension in these muscles and allow it to flow out. You may notice your shoulders drop slightly as you let the muscles relax. Now travel down your upper arms, your lower arms, hands, all the way to the tips of your fingers. Feel the relaxation spread down your arms as any tension flows out on the air as you exhale. (The therapist continues down the body mentioning each part and allowing time for the breathing to carry the tension away.)

(The therapist next provides *cue breathing*.) You are very relaxed and comfortable now. I am going to give you a cue so that your body will remember and go back to this state of relaxation should you be in a situation that is stressful for you. Notice that when you breathe in, the air is cool on your nose and throat; when you breath out, the air is warm. Focus on the sensations . . . cool air in . . . warm air out . . . Let these sensations become connected in your mind with the good feelings of calm and relaxation you are feeling right now. Know that the next time your mind focuses on the cool and warm your body will remember and respond with relaxation and calm. Spend a few minutes now focusing on the cool and warm, enjoying the relaxation (several minutes of silence). When you are ready, return slowly to the here and now, knowing that you will be alert and refreshed but will carry relaxed feelings with you for the rest of your day.

Practicing the relaxation exercises when the individual is not under immediate stress is important. Little benefit is gained by the client trying to relax when the drive to binge is already strong. Ideally, the relaxation sequence should be practiced twice a day for 15 minutes each time. The client may have difficulty maintaining relaxation for that long at first and may need to work up to it. After several weeks of practice, the client can usually maintain the response by practicing once a day.

Some clients respond well to combining imagery with the relaxation sequence. In addition to the recording of the relaxation instructions, the therapist may want to give the client a pre-recorded imagery tape which will assist by having the client go, in her mind, to a special place. The wording on the tape in the therapist's voice may be similar to the following.

Imagery Exercise. "While you are in this relaxed, peaceful state, I want you to take a brief vacation. In your mind, I want you to go to a special place. It may be one that is in your life now or it may be one you remember from your past. It may even be one you create entirely from your own imagination. In any case, it will be a place with good feelings connected to it, feelings of being comfortable, relaxed, and happy.

Go there now and really look around. Notice the colors and shapes around you. The light may be bright or dim. See things around you, noticing the details of your special place. As you are looking around your special place, notice also the textures. Are the things around you rough or smooth, hard or soft? If you would like, in your mind, reach out and touch something and feel its texture.

Notice the temperature of the air. Is it warm or cool? If there are any sounds you associate with your special place, let them come into your experience. Listen and notice small sounds and louder sounds. Let them come back into your awareness so your special place will be complete.

If there is anything you would like to do while you are here, feel free to do that in your mind now. If not, just continue enjoying your special place a few more minutes. Know that when you return to the here and now, you will bring with you the calm, relaxed feelings you have now and that they will stay with you as you go on with whatever your day requires of you."

If the therapist has identified a special place prior to making this tape, he/she can make the instructions even more specific. For example, if the client's favorite place is the beach, the therapist can include reference to the sound of waves and sea gulls, the smell of salt water, the feel of the breeze and the sand under your feet, and so forth. One client, Ruth, had a special place that was a garden in which she used to play as a child. Ruth had a highly developed visual sense, indeed she was a talented artist. Because of this, we included many visual references to the colors of things in the garden, the grass, rocks, sky, roses that bloomed there, and so forth. Ruth reported that her most difficult time of the day was right after coming home from work. She would be tired and feeling rushed to get dinner started. This was also a very heavy binge period for her. She began using the tape to help her unwind at the end of her work day and to ease the transition into responsibilities at home. On the days that she did this, she noticed that the amount she consumed in her evening binge was less and she was vomiting less.

As the client becomes more comfortable with the relaxation exercise, a helpful method is to have her practice the cue breathing and imaging for a few minutes several times during the day. This helps combat the gradual build up of tension that accumulates as the day goes on. Many of the women with bulimia are unaware of sensations in their bodies, so they do not notice the build-up of tension until it is at a high level. As Kathy put it, "All of a sudden I will notice that I am clenching my fists and jaws and that my shoulder muscles really ache. Until it gets to this point, I am not aware of it." In addition to providing a release of tension, the relaxation training will help increase the woman's awareness of physical sensations in her body.

Case of Jill

Many women with bulimia describe a feeling of aimlessness in their lives. They often are lacking clear career goals even if they are enrolled in college, employed full time, or even in professional school. A definite lack of direction and purpose exists in their lives. Some of this comes from genuine confusion. They may have been in such a pattern of trying to do what others wish in order to gain approval that they have difficulty formulating their own goals. They have difficulty in decision making.

This was expressed by Jill when she stated, "I went to college because that's what the kids did in my family. I majored in chemistry first, probably because both my parents are chemists. Then I changed to geology which was what my boyfriend was studying. After college, I came home and drifted between jobs for a year. I no longer dated my boyfriend so I didn't have him to follow. I feel like a total failure because I wasn't what everybody wanted me to be, although I was never quite sure what that was, anyway. I am, just now, at age 23, starting to try to figure out what I want to do with my life and it's really hard. I find myself asking lots of people what they think I should do. I never had any practice making up my own mind. It's not that may parents were overbearing, but they managed to subtly tell you that what you suggested wasn't what they wanted. Like constantly asking, 'Are you sure that's what you want to do.'''

Jill's parents would continue to question her until she was so filled with doubts that she gave up on her decision. This pattern was followed seemingly on virtually all decisions from, "I think I want to go back to graduate to school," to "I would really like to own a kitten." During several months of counseling, Jill had managed, against much opposition, to move out of the family home and rent her own apartment. To help her decide on some goals for her life, she took a series of part time jobs that gave her hands on experience in areas in which she was interested. She also enrolled in two graduate level courses that gave her the confidence that she could do graduate work and also filled pre-requisite requirements in one of her areas of interest. Working together, the client and counselor investigated graduate programs that would fill Jill's needs. Jill selected one in a city where some of her college friends had settled. She applied and was accepted. She requested that the counselor be present when she told her mother of her decision. A joint session was arranged.

In the joint counseling session with her mother, the scenario was played out in full. Jill informed her mother of her decision. The mother's response was typical of their script. She repeatedly questioned whether Jill was sure. When Jill assured her that she had given it a great deal of thought, the mother began pointing out all the ways it could fail, including the fact that, "With you in another state, there is no way your father and I could bail you out, if you get into trouble." When this did not produce the desired wavering in the decision, the mother proceeded to remind Jill of all the ways she had "failed" in the past, and how many times she had disappointed her father. (The father was not present at this session.) This last attack produced tears and confusion in the client, but she hung onto her decision.

Throughout the session, she made frequent eye contact with the therapist for reassurance. The therapist had to intervene several times during the session to support the client. The statements by the mother were labeled as "sincerely caring about her daughter but not realizing how much the daughter had grown up." The mother was reassured that Jill had visited the college and talked to professors in her chosen field. They had reviewed her transcripts and encouraged her to apply. Jill had even checked out the availability of therapy groups to continue getting help with her bulimia. The reassurance did little to comfort the mother who resorted to repeating all of her previous statements of why Jill's decisions wouldn't work. She continued her attempts to regain control of her daughter's life in the few weeks remaining before Jill left. She gradually became resigned to the fact that Jill was leaving but let her know that "she could always come home if she failed."

How Can the Therapist Teach Decision-making Skills?

In working to help develop decision-making skills, the therapist will need to be aware of the client's high need to make the "right" decision. Even small decisions may be agonized over or completely avoided. The therapist will need to emphasize that, "Deciding not to decide is, in itself, a decision." He/she may need to point out that decisions rarely are "set in concrete" and small ones may often be changed with little lost except time. The therapist will point out that something is learned from each decision regardless of the outcome. For example, when Jill was choosing which courses to take to help her career decision, she found that she gained valuable information by considering those areas in which she thought she had an interest even when she discovered after consideration that she hated the area. By deciding to take the courses, she gained valuable information needed to make the bigger career decision.

Sometimes the decision can be facilitated by considering "What is the worst thing that could happen if this doesn't work out?" and "What will happen if you make no decision at all?" Often, the individual is most concerned about looking foolish or having failed. This is likely to be the way "wrong" decisions were treated in her family when she was a child. She may need help realizing that she is an adult now and no longer has to go by her family's definition of a "right" decision. Standard decision making techniques such as writing down and weighing alternatives should be instituted. Often, the individual tries to complete the process entirely in her head resulting in a great deal of preoccupation and anxiety.

Another contributing factor to the inability to make decisions is what might be termed the "cripple mentality." Women who have bulimia often deny themselves opportunities, feeling that "I can't do that because I am bulimic." The counselor needs to confront this reasoning and emphasize that feeling better about oneself comes *before* the bulimia goes away. For example in the case of Jill mentioned previously, her decisions to find her own apartment, take graduate courses, change jobs, and eventually obtain her masters degree were all positive steps towards recovery from her eating disorder. As each decision was approached, her binging and purging initially increased as her anxiety level rose. The fear of failure was almost enough to cause her to avoid decision making entirely. The decision making had to begin with small matters of little impact. These small decisions were necessary because they posed little threat and helped to build Jill's confidence. As each decision was made, she experienced feelings of elation and pride in herself. The drive to binge and purge reduced markedly and feelings of really being in control of her life developed. She was not completely free of bulimia when she left town, but she had made considerable progress in her recovery. Her feelings of aimlessness, and therefore worthlessness, had diminished and were being replaced by a new confidence and sense of purpose.

At times, the therapist may sense that an investment exists in continuing the pattern of "wrong" decisions. In Jill's case, for instance, thinly veiled statements were made by her mother that her caring was conditional on Jill needing her help. Although the client may intellectually agree to the importance of independent thinking, an emotional need to stay dependent may remain. Also the unspoken thought "If I remain incompetent, no one will expect anything of me" may interfere with making decisions.

In one of the final counseling sessions before Jill left for school, her therapist asked her to list the ways in which she could sabotage her success at school, if she chose to do so. (Emphasizing that it, of course, *is a choice*.) She listed ways such as "I could become very lonely and really dwell on how much I miss my parents and friends." "I could become depressed and stop attending classes." "I could become so afraid of failure that I could avoid formulating an idea for my thesis." For each statement, she was helped to generate a way that she could actively help herself avoid having that alternative occur. The list, along with the coping skills was written out for her to take with her.

How Does Keeping
a Journal Help?

Clients with bulimia have difficulty acknowledging something which they did well or about which they felt good. The counselor must emphasize the importance of discovering what they do right and what they do that gives good feelings as well as what depresses them.

By sitting down and recording the day's events and feelings, the client may begin to distinguish repeated behaviors that upset her. For example, Laura noticed that she felt depressed whenever she entered her closet to decide what to wear. Many of her clothes were from a time in her life when she had a long illness which kept her weight at 20 pounds lower than her present, healthy weight. Several times a week, she would try on clothes she knew wouldn't fit and then feel depressed. Laura decided, entirely on her own, to hold a garage sale and got rid of everything that didn't fit. This issue also presented the opportunity to discuss her "magical thinking" that "As soon as I lose weight and can wear these clothes again, everything will be wonderful and I will no longer have bulimia."

The journal can also be useful to remind the client of things that helped in the past. Set backs commonly occur during the course of therapy. Being able to go back and re-read how they helped themselves the last time they felt down can be very helpful.

Can Assertiveness
Training Assist?

Bulimic clients are often heavily invested in being liked and gaining approval. They have little experience in asking for what they want or need. They may seethe inside when someone takes advantage of them but will rarely complain. Standard principles of assertiveness training can be very helpful. Helping the client distinguish between assertive and aggressive behavior is important. The overall message is that, "You are a worthwhile person, it is appropriate for you to ask to have your needs met. You do not always have to be placating others to be liked."

Many books are available on this subject. Two that are helpful are *Why Do I Feel Guilty When I Say No?* by Manuel Smith and *Your Perfect Right* by Alberti and Emmons.

Is Talking to Friends Recommended?

A common source of coping of which bulimic clients have difficulty in availing themselves is talking to or calling a friend. Because they view their eating habits as "disgusting," they often fear rejection from others if it should become known. This fear was expressed by one client who said "As soon as I start to really get to know someone, I pull away. I'm afraid they will find out my secret and think I am weird or disgusting."

Although the client may describe herself as having many friends, a closer look shows that several people may tell her their problems and come to her for support, however, she rarely, if ever, returns the sharing. By failing to share information about herself, the situation may develop where individuals who would like to be her friend drift away because "I never really got to know her." Those that stay are frequently dependent individuals who take advantage of the client's needs to gain approval by giving to others. The result of this pattern is that the woman develops the feeling that "Friends are people who take advantage of you." She may pull back completely from having friends. She often feels isolated because of this and may be very lonely.

The therapist can help the client explore her feelings about different friends and their personalities as viewed by the client. She can then explore with whom she could share what about herself. The therapist will help her learn how to share and to recognize the benefits received. Talking to friends necessitates being assertive, thus learning the assertiveness skills may be a prerequisite. One of the best ways of learning this type of interaction is in group therapy with other women who have bulimia.

CHAPTER 9

PHYSICAL EXERCISE: A COMPONENT OF TREATMENT

Within the treatment program, exercise serves two purposes: first, as a way to help clients cope with stress and second, as an aid in controlling weight. With many of our clients, regardless of their other problems, if stress and tension are present and they are physically able we encourage them to begin an exercise program. We have found that exercise is a simple and effective means of stress reduction. The stress may be long term and chronic such as a demanding boss or situational such as an argument with a spouse. Besides helping the client relax and lower her tension level, we have observed that a regular program of exercise helps alleviate depression.

How Much Exercise
Is Recommended?

Staying on a regular exercise program is difficult for clients, particularly when they are first getting started. Unfortunately most people stop exercising for a variety of reasons. If the client can be encouraged to stay on an exercise program for six months, the program is likely to become a standard part of her daily schedule. That means that the therapist must be not only persistently supportive but help the client find activities that are pleasant (at least to a degree) and which can be fitted into a daily schedule. We recommend the exercise decided upon be done at least three times a week, for 20 minutes each time and make the point that five times a week would be even better.

What Exercises
Are Suggested?

Activities that we suggest as possibilities are (1) a brisk walk, (2) jogging, (3) swimming, (4) bicycling, (5) aerobic dance, or (6) some sport like tennis or handball. Included in a program of exercise should be some warm up and stretching calisthenics to help the client stay flexible and help prevent injury from the more strenuous activities.

Does Exercise Help
in Weight Loss?

While we are convinced of the effectiveness of exercise as a technique for combatting stress and depression,   use of exercise as an aid in weight loss presents us with a slightly different problem. As we have been stressing in this book, for those persons concerned with what they see as excess weight, going on a highly restrictive diet is not a permanent or a healthy way to lose weight. This leads naturally to the question, besides reorienting their attitude toward what is an appropriate weight, what else can the person concerned with weight do? While nothing that we know of will help individuals meet the unrealistic standards of society that are presented in the media, an appropriate exercise program does hold out some hope for many overweight and normal weight individuals who would like to weigh less. A program of exercise, of course, will only work to the extent that it is in keeping with the biological potentials of the individual involved. Evidence shows that exercise used wisely can help to reset, to some degree, the body's set-point.

The amount of body fat a person has, regardless of sex or age, is significantly affected by a program of prescribed exercise. People who stop exercising, or who reduce their level of physical activity, find that their body fat increases even if they reduce the amount they eat. Miller and Sims (1981) found that exercise helped patients in their program who had been able to make large reductions in their weight keep the weight off. Brownell (1982) gave five reasons why exercise is important as a way to help individuals lose weight. These reasons are that exercise (1) increases energy expenditure, (2) counteracts the ill effects of obesity, (3) suppresses appetite, (4) increases basal metabolism, and (5) minimizes the loss of lean tissue.

Brownell's conclusions are supported by a variety of research studies on the effects of exercise upon weight. For example, Thompson, Jarvie, Lahey, and Cureton (1982) cited studies to show that exercise produces an increase in the metabolic rate that outlasts the actual duration of the exercise. That is, a person expends energy not only during the exercise period, but his/her metabolic rate remains about 10% above the basal rate for up to 48 hours after strenuous exercise. One of the factors that relates to metabolic rate and energy expenditure is the amount of lean body mass that the individual has. A program of regular exercise can increase an individual's lean body mass. This is important in weight reduction because lean body mass (LBM) is approximately three times more metabolically active than fat tissue (Thompson et al., 1982).

The most practical and impactful approach to take advantage of this fact is to set up a program of moderately strenuous exercise for periods of 15 to 20 minutes 4 to 5 times a week (Sharkey, 1975). Sharkey found that this program of activity not only used up considerable energy but also decreased food intake significantly. If the amount of exercise is increased to two hours daily, the person's food intake goes back up to the level it was when the person was sedentary. For even longer periods of exercise (2 to 6 hours) food intake increases to a level that keeps weight constant. The effect of exercise and its limitations in controlling weight needs to be stressed and restressed with clients with bulimia, since many of them seem to believe that if a little of something is good, a lot will be even better. In their striving for perfection, they push themselves and, without someone monitoring their behavior, they may exercise too much for their own best interests.

Thompson et al. (1982) summed up the findings on the effects of exercise as follows:

1. Obese individuals who exercised lost significantly more weight than did nonexercising obese and exercising or nonexercising controls.

2. Superior weight loss was shown for those exercising 4 to 5 times per week as compared with those exercising less frequently.

3. Significant differences in fat loss existed between exercising and control groups. Heavy persons lost significantly more fat than did thin persons.

Wardle and Beinart (1981) agreed with the previous statements and added that exercise produces as much weight loss as dieting and that a combination of the two is even more effective. These two authors warned against planning much dieting with a person who has a history of binging but suggested that some change of eating patterns can take place without causing additional problems.

Mayer, Roy, and Mitra (1956) found that exercise also alters the amount of energy which is expended in eating and digesting food. That is, in addition to the increase in metabolic rate from exercising, an increase occurs in the metabolic rate that follows eating. This is called the *thermic effect*. In normal weight subjects, exercise increases the thermic response to food by 17%. Obese subjects, however, do not show a similar effect from exercise. This suggests that obese individuals have not only a lower Basal Metabolic Rate but, also, a lower exercise-induced thermic response. The reader should keep in mind that normal body weight individuals do not have this lack of response to exercise and that, in spite of their feelings to the contrary, even persons with bulimia who feel they are grossly overweight are often well within normal weight limits for their height.

What About Exercise
for Women with Bulimia?

We have been suggesting that exercise must be used with caution with clients with bulimia. The therapists must be aware of the perfectionistic nature of these clients and their tendency to ritualize behavior. One client, Sally, who had been a competitive athlete, decided, "I must exercise at least 20 minutes each day." No exceptions were allowed, and when circumstances prevented her from exercising one day, she had "failed." This "failure" led to a sequence of self-deprecating thoughts which were followed by a binge and resolve to "try even harder from now on." At one point, she announced that she had signed up to compete in triatholon. This involved a race that combined running, canoeing and bicycling for a total of 100 miles. She had told all of her friends that she had signed up for it with the expectation that the threat of the embarrassment of having to tell them she dropped out would keep her training for the race. She had difficulty acknowledging the self-defeating nature of the bind in which she had placed herself.

A tendency also is present for these clients to begin competing with themselves. If they are running two miles a day and push themselves to two and one-half miles, that amount becomes the standard, and two miles is never good enough again. One client, Laura, measured her athletic conditioning by taking her resting pulse rate. As she progressed in her training, the pulse rate declined. She would take her pulse every morning and her day was ruined if her pulse was higher than the lowest previous reading. She was very happy if she set a new low reading but seemed to have no awareness that a physiological limit exists to how low her pulse could get. The only way she could win this competition would be for her heart to stop completely.

Despite these drawbacks, exercise can be used to help these clients. Moderation must be stressed and both the therapist and the client will need to monitor the client's tendency to compete with herself. Flexibility in scheduling the exercise is essential, however the client has a tendency to hear the scheduling aspect and to ignore the flexibility aspect that is so essential. Three times a week is good, five may be better, but more does not add anything of significance. To be of the most benefit the exercise periods need to be spread out over the week rather than have them all scheduled over the weekend. The therapist's credibility is strengthened if he/she practices what is being recommended. The client will frequently ask the therapist if she/she exercises. The therapist will need to be familiar with walking trails, gyms, and swimming pools in the area. Any information the therapist can supply to make starting easier will make exercising more likely to happen.

SUMMARY

Some closing thoughts on using exercise with clients with bulimia:

1. Katch and McArdle (1977) suggested that an exercise program begun early in life, before the adolescent growth period, may help prevent the development of excess fat cells.

2. Even when individuals have good reasons for staying in an exercise program, about 50% drop out. The therapist needs to be aware of the difficulty that clients have in staying with an exercise regiment. The challenge is to devise an acceptable and meaningful exercise program and help the client find ways to stay on the program.

3. Asking clients to exercise is not enough. Clients may need detailed instructions on how to do the particular activities or exercises. These instructions should probably be given both in writing and orally and, if possible, through demonstrations (Thompson et al., 1982).

4. When working with individuals who have bulimia the therapist needs to keep in mind our earlier caution that they, more than other clients, may need to have their activities monitored because of their tendency to strive for perfection. This can result in discouragement for the client when things do not work as she wishes and precipitate an intensification of the bulimic behavior.

CHAPTER **10**

GROUP THERAPY

Group therapy can be extremely beneficial for women with bulimia. Group therapy is not a replacement for individual therapy, but can enhance or extend work done in individual sessions. It may be used concurrently with individual work, may be added as the client becomes ready through individual therapy, or may be the sole treatment as individual work is phased out. Group membership can provide a valuable support system as well as a place to discuss problems with others who share the same issues. The individual with bulimia often behaves as though she bears a stigma, in other words, as if she would be rejected by others if they knew her secret. This unfortunate feeling of being stigmatized is shared by other groups in our society such as homosexuals, herpes sufferers and former mental hospital patients. Because all members of the group have bulimia, no need exists to guard the "secret" of their eating behavior. Members often express the feeling, "This is the one place I can come and truely be myself." First, we will look at factors that need to be considered in forming a therapy/self-help group for women with bulimia. Second, illustrations of the group interaction will be discussed to give the reader an idea of types of issues dealt with by the group.

**Who Is Qualified to
Lead Group Therapy?**

The therapy sessions should be led by a therapist who has been trained to understand and professionally facilitate group processes. Although lay-lead self-help groups can provide some of the aspects of support and commonality, some serious drawbacks can occur. Without some guidance, these groups may tend to stay with superficial discussions of eating behaviors. This does little to help with the underlying emotional issues that are so important. If material of high emotional impact should be revealed, such as child abuse, incest, or sexual concerns, the lay-leader and other group members may not have adequate skills to help the woman resolve some of the feelings that have been exposed. This can be especially difficult if the lay-leader is someone who has recovered from bulimia herself but may still be struggling with some of the same issues. To take the risk of disclosing these issues and then have them dropped with no resolution can be devastating to the client who discloses these feelings as well as to the other group members.

SCREENING GROUP MEMBERS

The group facilitator should screen all potential members in an individual session prior to admitting them to the group.

Are Women with Anorexia
Admitted to the Group?

Women with active anorexic symptoms should be excluded from the group and seen in individual therapy. The major reason for this exclusion is the competitiveness that is exhibited by women with anorexia. Exposure to another person whom they perceive as thinner than themselves, often results in an intense desire to diet. This can produce a "My lowest weight is lower than your lowest weight" competition that can be disastrous. Indeed one of the authors had the experience where two women with anorexia met in the office waiting room. They spent several uncomfortable moments eyeing each other and when they separated, each vowed to restrict food consumption even more strictly. One of the women stated, "When I saw that she was so thin, thinner than me, I was so jealous. I knew you were probably more worried about her than you were about me. I was angry and depressed and went home determined to diet even more strenuously."

Is Confidentiality
Discussed During Screening?

In the screening session, several issues need to be covered with the potential member. An important point is that nothing said within the group is to be shared outside the group setting. This rule of confidentiality addresses one of the major concerns of the new member. "What if I meet someone I know in the group?" Many clients have a fear that information about their bulimia will somehow be relayed to bosses, friends, and acquaintances whom they have worked so hard to deceive. They anticipate this resulting in considerable embarrassment and humiliation. The therapist will point out that "Even if you do know someone in the group, she will be just as anxious as you are to have confidentiality maintained. These women will understand completely your need to have information kept within the group."

Are Women Who Don't Purge
Allowed in the Group?

When interviewing potential members, no major attention is given to whether or not the person purges as well as binges. Some therapists and some clients will be concerned that women who don't purge will pick up the practice from other group members. This does not seem to happen for two reasons. First, most women with bulimia who don't vomit have considered it and have probably tried it. The gag reflex is either difficult for them to trigger or the practice is so aversive to them that they don't continue. Second, if a group member who does not purge attempts the behavior, the other group members exert a great deal of pressure on her to stop.

Is a Commitment to
Attend More Than One
Session Essential?

If the member is to enter an on-going therapy group, she needs to be encouraged to make a commitment to attend a minimum of three sessions before making a decision to drop out. When an individual attends only one session of a therapy group and then drops out, it is disruptive for the other members. Also the person cannot form an accurate impression of the group in one session. Sometimes the group may be very intense and serious and at other times a great deal of laughter and joking may take place. If the new member's first session is a very serious one, she may be threatened by the intensity. She needs to be given permission, in advance, to only participate to the extent at which she is comfortable. Some clients are shocked if their first session turns out to be one where joking occurs, especially if the joking is about bulimic behavior. One client expressed her feelings, "I was shocked to hear everyone laughing and making jokes about eating. I have been so ashamed of this part of myself that I didn't know how to react. In some ways, it was a relief to not take it so seriously but I wasn't quite sure how to react."

How Does the Therapist
Encourage New Members
to Join the Group?

Often directly addressing the ambivalence about becoming part of the group can help. The therapist might say "I know you have lots of doubts about being in the group. Most all of the members report having wanted to turn around a hundred times on their way to the first session. I guess, the first few times you will have to take my word that the group will be a positive experience."

An easier transformation for the group, and often for the client is to have more than one new member join at a time. The therapist may screen clients so as to have two or more enter an on-going group together. The new members may benefit from what the group has achieved and the group members may benefit from the fresh approach of the new members.

STRUCTURING THE GROUP

What Is the Group Leader's Role?

Generally, a good idea is for the therapist to explain the role of the facilitator in the group. The therapist may state "One of the things that may surprise you is that I don't talk a lot in the group. The major focus will be on the members sharing and helping each other. I will be there to help by keeping the group working on the issues. If someone talks about a topic that is very emotional for her, I will help her explore the issue and aid in resolving some of her feelings so that she will not feel unfinished when she leaves the session. I also will move in to protect any member who is being pressured by other group members to reveal more of her feelings than is comfortable for her." This last point, pressure from other group members, rarely occurs; however, it is frequently a concern of entering members.

Are Individual Sessions Interwoven with Group Sessions?

Frequently the therapist is wise to set up a system so the group members can arrange for individual sessions as needed if they are not being seen in a one-on-one therapy. This can be referred to as a "therapist on demand" schedule in which an individual session can be arranged as the need arises. Being able to see the therapist between group sessions is important because issues of intense emotional impact come up in the group session. Although the person may seem to have worked through the problem in the group, it can surface again several days later resulting in intense feelings of depression or anger. Rather than have the client struggle with the problem until the next group session, the client should be seen during the week between meetings. This does not seem to rob the group of momentum or cohesion, and considering the potential for severe depression, is well worth the therapist's time.

Are New Members Paired
with On-going Group Members?

When one or more new members are added to an on-going group, a helpful tactic is to pair members with more established members as a "sponsor" or "big sister." This gives the new person someone with whom to associate and reduces the temptation to drop out of the group.

ADVANTAGES OF GROUP THERAPY

What Are Some Advantages
to Joining a Group?

Several things can be accomplished in group therapy that cannot take place in individual sessions. Just meeting other people who have the same problem can be very therapeutic. Despite frequent magazine and newspaper articles, the woman with bulimia still may feel as though she is the only person who does this "awful behavior." When asked if she was anxious that she might know some of the group members, one teen replied, "Not really. None of the people I know would do this sort of thing." She was amazed to meet two of her high school classmates in the group. "I never would have guessed you two have bulimia. You always seem to have your act so together." Meeting other women with the same problem can be very normalizing. The cognition develops that "She doesn't seem so weird. Maybe I'm not as bad as I thought."

As mentioned earlier, women with bulimia tend to avoid close relationships because of fear of discovery of their "secret." This fear is bypassed in the group by the knowledge that everyone there has the same problem. This leaves the way open for the formation of close bonds between group members. An important step toward recovery seems to take place as a group member allows herself to reach out to other members and to accept their help. Most members are eager to help the others. After all, an important part of their identity is often their role as a "helper." A woman with bulimia finds more difficulty allowing someone else to give help to her.

One of the real advantages of having an on-going group into which new members are brought and others "graduate" as they recover is that members at a variety of stages of recovery are present. A reassuring point for a woman struggling to control her binge-purge episodes is that others have had to deal with the same feelings. "I was really afraid I would gain weight, too. I did gain a few pounds at first but now I'm the same." "I was really upset with myself when I went back to binging after I had gone two weeks without one. I had to remind myself that I hadn't gone more than two days for the last four years and focus on what I had accomplished not just that I had 'failed.'"

Another area where the group can be very helpful is in contesting magical thinking. "You are kidding yourself if you think the right man is going to solve your problems. I'm married to a great guy and I still have bulimia. I can lie there in bed beside him and still feel so damn alone." "I worked so hard to keep a 4.0 average in college. Now that I have graduated, nobody knows or cares and I still have bulimia even though I have the job I worked so hard for."

Group therapy offers several advantages that can enhance individual therapy. It is not a substitute for individual work, but does contain aspects that are impossible to achieve in one-on-one counseling. Sharing a common problem helps the women feel less alone. Being free to interact without having to protect a "shameful secret" allows friendships to develop. Allowing oneself to accept support, caring, and encouragement from others as well as to give it is a positive experience. Sharing intense feelings about parents or events in the past with others who understand can have a healing effect. Gina expressed her feelings, "A year ago, when I was in therapy with another counselor, I felt like the only person I could really talk to about my life and who understood me was someone I was paying to have listen. I always felt she wouldn't have listened either if I hadn't been paying her. Now with the group, I have six other people who are interested and understand me and are really rooting for me to recover."

The support and compassion shown among group members are helpful as the woman begins to face the emotional issues in her life and the underlying causal factors. The kind of support and compassion given by fellow members is unusual for women with bulimia and can initially be difficult for her to accept. The role of support giver is much more familiar and comfortable. The facilitator may need to encourage her to accept the caring offered by other members without the suspicion that "they must want something from me."

SELF-CRITICISM

Is Self-criticism Common?

In a new group, the first sessions are often devoted to "confession" of the behavior. This can lead to telling "war stories." "If you think that was bad, let me tell you about the time I . . ." A certain amount of this is helpful to establish commonality among the group members; however, the group facilitator must guide members toward discussing issues that are underlying the behavior. As the hesitation diminishes and the level of the material disclosed becomes more intimate, negative feelings about their bodies are brought out. Often, the others are surprised to hear a member describe herself as "too fat" or having enormous thighs. Comments disputing this self-description are generally disregarded by the member making the complaint. The therapist needs to point this out and perhaps comment that they all are much more critical of themselves than are others. This can lead to a more important discussion about "Why is it that it is so important to have a 'perfect' body?" and "What are the consequences of continually putting yourself down because your body is not perfect?"

Are Compliments
Difficult to Accept?

Feelings of lack of worth and inability to feel satisfaction about accomplishments are brought out. Women in the group may try to give positive feedback to one of the members only to find that the compliments are negated. One member brought samples of some pictures of wildflowers she had painted in water colors. As the members admired them, she pointed out how they "could have been better," and how she had "done better ones in the past." Finally, the group leader pointed out, "Ruth, Sharon just gave you a compliment. Can you stop criticizing yourself long enough to accept it?" Sharon pointed out that she had felt annoyed and somewhat rejected by Ruth's avoidance of her comments. This kind of avoidance of positive feedback is common and needs to be gently confronted.

Can the Group Help Overcome
the Self-Denial of Success?

As the group progresses, often the members begin to recognize how they have a tendency to discount successes. For example, Elaine stated, "Here I am, about to graduate from college. I have already been accepted to graduate school in the area I really want to study. I am getting lots of positive feedback from my professors about my work. Yet all I can think about are things I could have done better and how I will probably screw up graduate school." The old parable about whether a glass with water in it is half full or half empty seems to apply to this type of thinking. The individual is seeing the glass as half empty, in other words, only focusing on what is missing or not there and ignoring what is present. At this point, a discussion of "What is so threatening about allowing yourself to see yourself as a success?" often brings out the fear that "If I ever relax and acknowledge that I have done well, I may quit working altogether. It is only the constant nagging of my internal critic that keeps me going." The therapist can help the group members work through this self-denial of success. Often group therapy can achieve this better than individual sessions for women with bulimia.

PERSONAL ISSUES

Are Troubles with Parents
and Siblings Discussed?

As comfort with taking risks in the group develops, negative feelings toward parents may be expressed. A teenager, Cindi, commented, "I like to come to group to talk about feelings because if I talk about them at home with my parents, somehow, I'm wrong and they are right. My mother has a 'prerecorded message' ready for every topic. It drives me nuts."

Elaine stated, "I never could do anything well enough for my father. He always had a criticism ready for anything I ever accomplished. It is really his voice that I hear when I pick apart things I do well." Anger may be expressed at their parents for expecting too much. Clair commented, "I was the oldest. I bought the younger kids clothes and fixed most of their meals. I was the one who helped with their homework. Where was my mother? I don't really know. All I know was that if I didn't do it, it didn't get done. I never want to have kids. I feel like I have already raised a family."

When the issues around parents are discussed, a common occurrence is for physical and emotional abuse to be described. Sharon recalls, "My two brothers and I were always in trouble. Looking back on it, we didn't do anything different from other kids our age but my father had such a bad temper. We were beaten with a belt at least once a week. You always wanted to be first if we were going to get it. That way you didn't have to watch the others get punished. Also, if one of them tried to squirm away, that made Dad madder and he was worse with the next one. It wasn't until I was in therapy that I really knew other kids weren't afraid of their fathers. Although I do remember wishing some of my friends' parents could be my parents. I'm really struggling with this whole issue now. I have some very angry feelings toward both my parents because my mother could have stopped some of it but she didn't even try. I also feel guilty for some of my negative feelings about them."

Another member, Kathy added, "My mother never hit us. She would stop talking to us for days. She would go to her green chair in the back room and sit and cry or stare into space. It would go on like this until whomever she was mad at would go back and apologize. I would rather she had hit us and gotten it over with. I can remember having a stomach ache for days when she was like this. I would wake up in the morning and feel terrible and it would take me a few minutes to remember why my stomach was in a knot. After awhile, I would apologize for anything, whether I was wrong or not, just to end the silence."

Many of the members can relate to the tales of emotional and physical abuse from their own experiences. They do a great deal to reassure the victim that no behavior they could have done would have warranted that type of punishment. This helps alleviate the feelings that "I must have been bad to have been treated that way."

SEXUAL TRAUMAS

Can Group Therapy Help with Sexual Traumas?

Sometimes a member will reveal sexual trauma to the group. Gina disclosed, "When I was nine, my grandfather raped me. We were all down at the lake swimming. When we were in the water, he pulled my bathing suit down and did it to me. I didn't know what he was doing until he had done it. I felt so dirty. I told my mother. All she said was that she would take care of it. As far as I know, nothing ever happened. We still went over there, like we always had. He never had intercourse with me again but there was a lot of touching and I was always afraid. I tried my best to see that he was never alone with my little sister."

Gina's statements opened the door for Cindy to reveal that she had been raped when she was eighteen. "I rented an apartment that I found out later had been previously rented by a drug dealer. One night two men broke in looking for him and drugs. When they found out he wasn't there, they were really angry. They raped me and left."

As one might imagine, disclosures about parental abuse, incest, and sexual assault are accompanied by strong emotion and tears. At this point, the facilitator should help the woman fully express her feelings. A strong tendency emerges for the group members to want to reassure and comfort the speaker prematurely and thereby shut down her expressions of pain. This is motivated by a sincere desire to give sympathy but also because the topic may be too close to their own inner most secrets and is causing them great discomfort. The group leader must pay special attention to anyone in the group who appears to be reacting with especially strong intensity to the disclosure and encourage them to express their feelings also.

GROUP SUPPORT

How Do Group Members
Show Support?

The group invariably gives strong support to a member who reveals painful information. The compassion and understanding expressed often goes a long way toward soothing some of the pain and guilt. Cindy related "I never was able to talk about the rape after it happened. My parents knew but it was so obviously painful to them that I never wanted to hurt them by bringing it up. I went through the police investigation but they never did find anything. I have felt dirty and awful about myself since it happened. I have always had the fear that if people knew, they would reject me. The boyfriend I had at the time couldn't deal with it and left me." The group gave her much reassurance that she was not damaged or dirty and that they cared a great deal about her. In later sessions, she told the group that their support had given her the courage to tell her fiance about the rape. She had felt that not telling him was creating a barrier between them but she had been too afraid of rejection to take the risk. He responded in a very compassionate and understanding manner which brought them even closer together. As result of the positive reaction of others, Cindy's negative feelings about her body were much diminished and her bulimia began to improve.

The group was also very supportive to Gina when she disclosed the incestuous assault by her grandfather. In addition to support and concern, the group encouraged Gina to confront her mother with her seeming indifference to the incident and ask her why she didn't do more about it. Gina spent quite a bit of time thinking about this and discussing with the group various ways she might approach her mother. She reported back to the group, "I asked my mother if she remembered my having told her about Grandfather. At first she denied any memory of it and tried to change the subject. As I persisted, she became angry and said, 'You think you had it so bad. You only had it happen to you once. I had to deal with it over and over. I tried to make sure you were never alone with him but I couldn't always manage.' She then refused to discuss it further and left the room."

At first, Gina felt devastated by the interaction but gradually began to sort through it. "I finally realized a lot of things about my mother; that she was a victim too, why she was so cold to my father, why she didn't touch us much as kids. All those things started to make sense. I'm still angry that she didn't protect me, especially since she knew he was that way. I also realize that I will never get the kindness and understanding from my mother that I have been yearning for all these years. She isn't capable of giving it. I gave it my best shot and it didn't work."

Gina then decided to talk to her mother's sister to try to answer some of her remaining questions. "I never really knew Aunt Louise very well but I decided that I had come this far, I might as well risk this too. It was interesting, she seemed to know why I had come before I said anything. She knew I was looking for information to try to understand Mother better. When I told her about the rape, she gave me the reaction I had hoped for from my mother. She put her arms around me and said, 'How awful that must have been for you.' We talked for five hours and I came away understanding both my mother and father better. I have always felt distant from my father because of his drinking but now I understand more why he may have had a drinking problem. Also, I realize now that mother came between Dad and us kids, probably because of her own father. I think I may be about ready to try a talk with my Dad next."

How Can the Therapist Help
the Individual Accept the
Group Support?

The group leader must be aware that even if the group is very supportive and caring toward the individual making these disclosures, the member may have second thoughts about having revealed such a personal part of themselves. At this point the therapist probably will offer to set up an individual session within the next few days. Also immediately following the group meetings the therapist should spend a few minutes alone with the woman to let her know that the therapist recognizes that sometimes after someone has talked about something as intimate as what she revealed today, that person feels vulnerable and may consider dropping out of the group. The client needs to be reassured that coming to the next session is very important and that by so doing she will be able to see how her disclosure has been accepted by the others and how it will not be used to hurt her. A woman with bulimia has difficulty in trusting others, in believing that they will not misuse private information. Often the trust can be built only over an extended time period. Also the development of that trust over time is needed for her to feel comfortable with the knowledge that others know such personal things about her.

The stages of disclosure should not be rushed, and the therapist must make sure that the group does not force the client to disclose too much too soon. The development of an acceptance and awareness of the intimacy and supportiveness of the group is crucial in order for the person to not feel vulnerable when offering personal information and sharing private feelings.

Do Members Ever
Get Discouraged?

As the group progresses, a stage develops where discouragement is expressed. "I've been coming for eight weeks now and really feel like I've been trying but I am still binging." This is the point where the group deals with the magical thinking that group therapy will accomplish recovery for them. After acknowledging this wish members really seem more able to accept responsibility for their behavior. Having accepted this responsibility, progress can now begin, however both therapist and client need to recognize that the progress will be slow.

Do Group Members Support One
Another Through Telephone Calls?

In every group, a point emerges where members spontaneously exchange phone numbers with the expressed intent to "call someone if you are having a hard time and need a friend." Invariably, in the next session, a group member reveals that she had a difficult time during the week. The other members chorus, "Why didn't you call one of us?" After a few weeks go by, the members start calling each other but only when they feel good. The group facilitator needs to point this out and emphasize that, "If you are feeling bad and are wanting to binge, try calling one of the group members. If, after you talk to someone, you still need to binge, go ahead and binge." The group members often express that they had felt that if they called someone, they couldn't binge or it meant they had failed. Giving each group member permission to try an alternative coping skill without making them feel like it must replace the binge is essential for her to feel that she has some control and has not lost it by telephoning.

Do Social Contacts Increase
as a Result of Group Therapy?

Social contacts between members outside the group are encouraged. The members may agree to begin an exercise program together. Having a friend with whom to swim or walk more likely will make them continue the activity. Often the members go out to eat together after a group meeting. This can be very helpful in making the process of eating with others a normal event and in overcoming the difficulties some members have of eating in public places. Occasionally, two members may develop a habit of binging together. This can be detrimental because often the partner who wants to binge can talk the other into participating even if she is not in the mood at the time. This should, of course, be strongly discouraged.

Do Members Help Each Other
Reach Out, Explore Alternatives?

Group members frequently encourage each other to take risks and make changes in their lives. Diane, a social worker, had a job where she worked exclusively with terminal cancer patients. She realized that she was coming home from work each day feeling depressed. Her binges generally took place immediately after returning home from work. She had little energy for social life and had given up most of the activities she used to enjoy such as jogging and sewing. The group helped her explore her feelings of failure at not wanting to stay with her job and feelings of guilt about leaving her clients and her co-workers. They also helped her overcome her hesitancy to apply for other positions because of fear that "no one will want me." Diane sent out resumes and found a job in another city where she would be working with adoptions. A member working on this type of issue often promotes the discussion by other members about their fears of failure and their avoidance of taking risks in their own lives.

SUMMARY

Group therapy can be a valuable component in the treatment of bulimia. Consideration needs to be given to the screening of new members. The group facilitator will need to clearly define his/her role in the group interaction.

The group offers the opportunity for members to develop a support system of individuals who share similar feelings and problems. Participation is a rewarding growth experience for both clients and therapist.

CHAPTER 11

FAMILY ISSUES
IN
THERAPY

Dear Mom and Dad

I'm sitting in the kitchen wondering how much longer you're going to stay mad at me. I can't take it much longer. I hurt so much that I feel the tears in my throat.

Why won't you talk to me? Why do I feel like I have to apologize before you'll even release some of your hostility? I feel so resented. I'm not going to apologize because it seems I always bear the guilt. I'm not going to take back what I said the other night either. Why am I not allowed to feel and express my hurt and anger? Why can't you love, me and feel sorry for me? I hurt so bad; I'm crying right now. Is it ever going to end? Will I ever feel/be loved by you again? How did this happen to us? I want to be happy. I want you to be happy. I love you and need to know you love me. I'm so scared. I'm at a loss as to how to express my love. Yes, I'm angry only because I feel like a failure and I want you to show me I'm not. I need to know that tomorrow, or in the future, I won't be a burden to you. I want to be a joy, not a bundle of sorrow.

Will everyone please stop trying to ignore my hurt and help me!?! I can't do it by myself. Will you please acknowledge that you're part of the problem so we can hurry and solve it because I hate waking up every morning only to realize that I hate waking up.

Do you realize how much I regret causing you grief? I want to feel like I can finally someday be happy. It has been hell pretending, it has been hell resenting, it has been hell seeking and seeking but never finding acceptance. Please love me and let me know you aren't going to hold the feelings I have and the pain that I feel against me. Quit making me feel like I'm weak and different and that I have a problem and all I need is to love myself more. I need to hear you say that I've been hurt, whether it was intentionally or not and that you love me despite my less than perfect ways, attitudes, and feelings.

Let me feel. Don't take this and make me feel like I'm the source of my own unhappiness. Don't make me feel like I brought this all upon myself.

I want so much for you all to be proud of me, but I only feel like a problem that you can't and perhaps don't want to relate to. I'm tired and very, very sad.

Your daughter,

Kathy

Rarely does a client have an eating disorder who doesn't have a conflicted relationship with at least one parent. This letter, written by a 17 year old client with bulimia, expresses the desperation and pain felt by these young women. The woman with bulimia has an intense need to be loved and she has a fear of rejection if she shows who she "really" is.

Kathy's family is typical of families of women with bulimia. Her father is a physician and her mother is a full time homemaker. She is the oldest female child, with three older brothers and a younger sister. Religion is a major focus in the family's life. Little personal freedom is allowed the children. If they disagree with the parents, they are told they are being "disrespectful." The mother tends to refuse to speak to Kathy after any disagreement, sometimes for several days at a time. The father is only peripherally involved with the raising of the children.

When Kathy was asked to describe the roles played by each of the children in the family, she stated, "My oldest brother is the 'brain.' He always got straight A's in school and will probably go to medical school. My second brother is the 'athlete.' He won letters in basketball and football and could have gone to college on an athletic scholarship. My next brother is the 'clown.' Everybody loves him because he's so funny. My sister is perfect. She not only gets straight A's but is a cheerleader and very popular at school."

When pushed to define her own role, Kathy had more difficulty. "I'm not sure where I fit in. I'm not as smart as the others, or as funny, and I'm no athlete. To be honest, I have always felt like I didn't fit in, in this family." As the discussion progressed, it became clear that one of Kathy's roles was that of the "listener." "Mom always has talked to me about the other kids and her problems. I only found out recently that she doesn't talk to any of the others this way." Her other role was as the "placator." Whenever disagreement occurred between other family members, Kathy was there to try to smooth things over.

FAMILY CHARACTERISTICS

The case of Kathy points up the fact that, whether the family members are personally involved in the therapy process or not, the counselor must be aware that family issues will be important and will come up repeatedly in both individual and group sessions. Before we proceed to a discussion of family interventions, let us look at the types of families from which these young women come. Not all of the characteristics described here will exist in all of the families but most will have several of these features.

The families seem to occupy either end of a continuum of closeness. Kathy's family represents the most frequent pattern and can be characterized as over-controlling and *enmeshed*. However, some families are at the other end of the continuum and are *chaotic* with little apparent involvement or interacting of the members.

What Are the Characteristics of the Enmeshed Family?

The surface appearance of this family is that of a typical two parent intact family. However, when a closer look is taken, the harmony in the family is seen to be superficial and misleading. The family is overly involved in each other's lives, especially the mother with the children. Very little privacy is allowed the children and the normal separation that is expected to occur in adolescence is stifled.

For example, Sharon described the situation in her family, "I am still living at home and I am 23 years old. If the phone rings my parents want to know who I am talking to and what they want. I can never leave the house without telling them where I am going and when I will be back. In the past, I know they opened my mail and searched my room. I wouldn't be surprised if they still do."

Kathy stated, "None of our bedroom doors have locks on them. If we go into our room and shut the door, you can count on it that there will be a knock on the door and Mom or Dad will want to know what is wrong." At another time Kathy said, "My parents are always wanting to know everything that is going on in our lives. They try to get each of us to inform on the others."

What Is Mother Like in an Enmeshed Family?

Cindi commented, "I think my mother really thinks I will turn into a juvenile delinquent if she isn't watching every minute. It is like you are constantly under suspicion. Then if I do do something wrong it confirms her worst fears. It gets so that I feel like I can hardly breathe sometimes."

The mother in these families is likely to be a full time homemaker, at least for the period when the children are young. They are often closely bonded to their children. In many cases the bonding is too close and enmeshed. These clients often express feeling responsible for their mother's well-being. Sometimes this comes from an awareness that children were somewhat of an unwelcome burden to the mother. Gina described, this, "I don't think my mother really liked kids. She probably wouldn't have had any if there hadn't been so much social pressure to have a family. I guess she kept on having kids (five) to prove to herself and others that she liked them."

Jill talked about her mother, "My mother dropped out of graduate school to marry my father. The doctor had told her that she couldn't have kids but she got pregnant almost right away. I was born just 10 months after my sister and I definitely wasn't wanted. I don't know why she had my brother three years later. In the last few years, after she finally returned to graduate school, my mother has been happier than I can ever remember."

Kathy reported that her mother had told her, "As a Christian woman, I am judged by how well my children turn out. I feel like I'm not a very good Christian when I think about your having bulimia."

What Is Father Like in an Enmeshed Family?

The father in these families is often a professional person; an engineer, physician, businessman, and so forth. When the client is asked to describe her father, she usually sees him as peripheral to the core of the family. He is heavily committed to his job and leaves much of the child rearing to the mother. He is involved in commenting on achievements of the children and in encouraging them to strive for even greater accomplishments but is not a part of their every day life. The women often make comments like, "I really don't know my father. The only times we are together for any length of time is on family vacations once a year. We really have a wonderful time for two weeks but then he disappears back into his work and I never see him. I don't know what I want from him or what I would have to say to him but something is missing."

What Kind of Expectations
Are Conveyed to Children
in Enmeshed Families?

Performance and achievement are expected from the children in these families. One sixteen year old high school sophomore, was apprehensive about bringing home her grade card. She expected to receive all A's and B's but, "Nothing I ever do is good enough for them. I know what they are going to say. 'This is very nice, dear, but couldn't you have done better in this subject if you'd tried harder?' They always find something that could have been better if I'd tried harder."

Although there are many messages of high expectations given to the children in these families, there are also doubts conveyed that they will ever achieve them. One daughter of a minister complained, "My mother is so concerned about how things will look to the congregation. 'What will people think?' is her constant worry. The only way I could please her is to be perfect at all times. I used to try a lot but now I just want to give up."

Decisions made by the young woman are frequently questioned. What if . . . (you get hurt, you get sick, you can't do it)? The constant implication is that, "You will probably fail." Gina stated, "I think my mother was trying to tell me she cares about me but what she actually said was something like, 'You've really taken on a lot of pressure; you've always been too emotional and sensitive. Don't be too disappointed if law school doesn't work out. Failing at law school is nothing to be ashamed of." After reflecting a while, Gina commented, "My mother took classes when I was growing up and threw herself into them totally. She always had to be the best. Somehow I feel like she wants me to succeed but not to be the best. Only she can be the best."

Donna described her father's reaction to her search for a new job. "You should stick to your old job. You are making good money. There are lots of people out there that don't have any job." When Donna applied for a new position and felt she had handled the interview well, her father's only comment was, "Don't get your hopes up."

What Are Characteristics
of the Chaotic Family?

In the chaotic family, very little notice is taken of the children. For example, Sally reported, "After my father died, my mother got really strange. She started dating men 20 years younger and dressed like a teenager. She almost totally ignored my brother and me. If it weren't for my older sister (who also had bulimia) we would not have had meals or clothes to wear. Mother never cleaned house or did any of the normal things mothers are supposed to do."

Lois stated, "My mother never liked the role of wife and mother. She stopped fixing meals when I was eleven. If you got hungry, you ate whatever was in the refrigerator. There were no curfews and we all came and went as we pleased. I tried to make things go better for the younger ones but I was just a kid myself."

Who Are "Irregular People?"
How Do They Hurt Women with
Bulimia?

Many of the women with bulimia have "irregular people" for parents. This concept is based on a book and tape by Joyce Landorf (1982) titled, *Irregular People*. On the cover of the book, Landorf describes this type of individual. "Irregular people are the ones who have the knack of wounding you every time you see them. They say the wrong thing, they ruin your day, they keep your emotions in constant turmoil. And an irregular person is someone you can't escape, usually a close relative—mother, father, husband, wife, brother, sister, or in-law. Irregular people have similar personality traits . . . You can't reason with them, can't depend on them, and can't expect any real support from them."

In the book, Landorf described irregular people as having a particular type of handicap. They are emotionally blind and deaf but only to certain people. They may be quite normal in their interactions with others and yet remain blind to some of the individuals closest to them. This blindness leads to inappropriate and often hurtful responses during interaction especially if it is emotional interaction. We can understand how this would be a problem when interacting with daughters. Let us give some examples of the type of irregular people who often are parents of clients with bulimia.

Sally, a 23 year old woman who was recovering from bulimia was told by her obstetrician that her pap smear test had come back reporting "suspicious cells." She went to her mother and told her, "Mom, I have to go into the hospital next week to have an operation on my cervix to remove these suspicious cells. I'm really afraid I may have cancer." Her mother replied, "That's too bad dear, oh, and remind me, I need to take the car in for an oil change next week." Sally was just crushed by her mother's lack of support but later realized, "I really shouldn't have expected anything else. She has never been any different." She went on to say, "What really hurts is that the kids my mother teaches in high school just love her. She always has time to listen to their problems and encourage them. When I was in high school, the kids used to tell me how lucky I was to have her for my mother." The concept of the irregular person helped Sally realize that her mother had a "handicap." Sally needed to know that she wasn't being rejected because something was wrong with her.

Another client, Terry, showed her mother pictures of the young man to whom she had just become engaged. Her mother remarked that, "Those really are ugly pictures. It's too bad he didn't have some decent ones taken." When Tina got upset at the remark, her mother couldn't understand her emotions and responded, "I was only being honest. Would you rather I lie?" One of the major concepts of the irregular person is illustrated by this interaction. The irregular person never admits that he/she is in any way at fault for the negative feelings in a relationship. The explanation is that the other person "took it wrong."

Sometimes individuals deal with the irregular person by making a joke out of their behavior. Gina remembers, "Every Saturday my mother would go to town to do the grocery shopping. While she was gone, my sister and I would clean the house from top to bottom. We would work so hard to get everything just right but invariably, my mother would find something we had missed. She never commented on how hard we had worked or how nice anything looked, just about the one thing left undone. It really hurt, but after a while my sister and I would take bets on how long it would take her to find something. I bet it would take less than five minutes. Lisa said it would be ten because she would be carrying in the groceries. I won."

Praise from the irregular person is either non-existent or conditional. "You did a nice job, but. . ." This kind of giving praise then taking it back gives the implied message that, "If you just try a little harder, maybe next time you will get my full approval." It is not difficult to see how this promotes the development of perfectionism and high needs for approval in these young women.

One of the major points made in the book by Landorf is that the irregular person never changes. You can change the way you deal with this person but he/she is unlikely to accept any responsibility for difficulties in the relationship and are therefore unlikely to change. Clients have a hard time giving up this hope that "one day my mother (or father) will finally see me and give me the acknowledgement that I am so hungry for." Sherry's story illustrates this point. Sherry was hospitalized for a serious heart problem unrelated to her bulimia. Her mother called her in the hospital and after talking a while, said that her father wanted to speak with her. Sherry's father had not spoken to her on the phone for over two years. He always listened on the extension but never said a single word. When Sherry heard that her father wanted to speak with her she thought, "Joyce Landorf, you are wrong. Irregular people can change. My father does love me after all and his wanting to talk to me proves it." When her father came on the line he only had one thing to say, "Well, Sherry, I guess this means you might need that plot in the cemetery before I do." Sherry reported later, "I was just devastated by his comment but what you had been saying finally got through to me. He never will give me the affection I would like to have from him. He isn't going to change. I feel sad about that but now I recognize I can give up running after it. Even though I haven't lived at home for ten years, I realize how much of my life I was determining because Daddy would approve or disapprove of what I was doing. It really doesn't matter anymore. He is never going to approve so I might as well do what I want for a change."

This letting go of the quest for approval from a parent can be a major step in recovery from bulimia. It is also a very confusing time for the client. They have been guiding their decisions by their internalized version of what the parent would want them to do for so long that they often have no idea what they want. The therapist must carefully avoid giving clues to what he/she would consider appropriate or the client might become dependent upon him/her to fill in for the parent.

Rarely is giving the book or the tape by Joyce Landorf to the irregular person useful in hopes that they will see themselves and reform. One client did give the tape to her parents without consulting the therapist. The parents, who were in the middle of a bitter divorce suit, listened to the tape. Each pointed to the other and exclaimed, "See, you are responsible for the trouble our daughter is having. If you had been a better father (mother) none of this would have happened." In truth, both were irregular people to their daughter but could only see the behavior in the other parent.

Can the Joyce Landorf
Book and Tape Be Helpful
in Therapy?

As therapists, we have found the tape to be particularly useful with clients with bulimia. The book is also helpful and because the book has a strong emphasis on Christianity, it can be very meaningful to those clients with a strong Christian faith. Other clients that do not share the religious views are more likely to be helped by the tape which has some references to Christianity but to much lesser degree than the book. The therapist will be wise to mention this to the client in advance of listening to the tape so that she does not feel that the therapist is promoting a particular religious point of view. We have used the tape in group sessions and found the result to be very impactful. Playing the tape often results in tears and emotional outpourings. Often, just having a label for the behavior and knowing you are not the only person who has struggled with an irregular person can be very helpful.

FAMILY INTERVENTIONS

Most of the families seen in therapy will be of the enmeshed type. Unfortunately, chaotic families are frequently resistant to becoming involved in counseling. Most of the women we have seen from chaotic families are older and have sought counseling on their own, sometimes many years after leaving home.

When Are the Parents Brought
into the Counseling Sessions?

The therapist needs to decide when to initiate family sessions When seeing a client who is over the age of 16, the therapist is advised to see the client individually for several sessions. Clients at that age are at the point of psychologically separating from the parents and often resist involving their parents in counseling. She must be reassured that nothing she says will be repeated to her parents and that, if the therapist does talk to them, the therapist will check with her first to determine what might be shared, if anything, with them.

Why Do Adolescents
Fear the Therapist?

Adolescents often approach seeing a therapist with the idea that the therapist is or will colaborate with their parents to "shape them up." This is especially true if the parents have discovered the purging behavior and have coerced the young woman into seeing the therapist. Sometimes seeing a "shrink" has been used as a threat. Other times, it has been conveyed to the client that seeing a therapist is an embarrassment to the family and is a form of failure.

What if Parents Are
Unavailable for Family
Sessions?

Frequently many women seeking treatment for bulimia have separated from their families of origin sometimes many years ago. Parents may live in another city or be deceased. In these cases, an important point for the therapist to realize is that family issues will still have to be approached and dealt with. For clients whose parents are unavailable, techniques such as expressing feelings while visualizing the parent in an empty chair, or writing letters (that are not sent) detailing hurt and angry feelings about events that occurred during their childhood can be used.

Do Parents Have Mixed Emotions
About Becoming Members of the
Counseling Sessions?

Yes, parents often have mixed emotions about being part of the therapy process. They frequently are concerned about their daughter's problems and may genuinely wish to help her recover. At the same time, they are invariably having considerable internal conflict over what role they and their parenting have played in her development of the eating disorder. Often parents have an anticipation that the therapist will point a finger at them and accuse them of being the cause of their daughter's problems. Other parents may choose the position that they are in the counseling sessions to collaborate with the therapist to change the daughter.

Considering the reluctance of both parents and women with bulimia to openly deal with the problem, the reluctance to seek help is not surprising and understandably many wait a long time before seeking help. Unfortunately, the young person may have been actively practicing bulimic behavior for several years before the family acknowledges the problem and talks to a physician or psychologist. Many of the young women work hard to conceal their behavior and will actively lie if asked about it. Others like Maxine told her parents that she was vomiting after eating. Her mother's reply was, "That's terrible! Let us know if you ever want to talk to someone about it." The subject was never brought up by the parents again and Maxine never worked up courage to face their disapproval a second time. In other families, like Sharon's, the parents were relieved to be contacted by her therapist for family sessions. They stated, "We have known what Sharon has been doing for two years but didn't have any idea what to do. Every time we approached her about it she would get very angry and we were afraid we would make it worse. We ended up saying nothing but we worry all the time."

**What Are Some of the First
Issues the Therapist Will
Discuss in Family Therapy?**

One of the issues that needs to be dealt with in the first session and repeated numerous times in later sessions is that of "Whose fault is this?" The best approach frequently is to have the therapist address the issue head on by saying to the parents, "You have both probably come here with several questions you want to ask about bulimia. Before we begin with those, let me spend a minute addressing the question you are both wondering but probably won't ask. My guess is that you are both wondering if you are going to be blamed for Leslie's (give the correct name of the person with bulimia) problems. Let me tell you a little about how I see this kind of situation develop. What we are dealing with is really a combination of two things. First we have a family with some problems in the ways they deal with each other. Second we have a child in the family who is extremely sensitive and intense. When this combination comes together, it can produce problems like Leslie has with bulimia. You have undoubtedly been doing the best job of parenting that you know how to do, and it may have worked well with your other children. For the type of intense personality Leslie has, we may need to work together to find other ways of parenting that can help her deal with her eating problems and feel better about herself."

This labeling of the parents as having had good intentions is important in assuring their cooperation as they are being asked to make changes later in the family therapy. In spite of the therapist's efforts, strong resistance to change may still be present. One father stated, "I'm 42 years old and I'm not going to change now." This kind of resistance must be met with the firm statement that "Some individuals with your daughter's problem die from the effects of it. At the very least, they can shorten their lives and damage their bodies. What you are willing or not willing to do in the way of change can have a great deal of impact on the outcome of her treatment."

Is the Family Attitude about Food and Eating Part of Family Therapy?

One of the first areas that needs to be discussed is the family's treatment of food. The enmeshed families may have engrained rituals about eating. In one family, the father was still pointing out to his children when they had enough or not enough on their plate. Everyone was still expected to finish everything on his/her plate whether he/she was hungry or not. One client said "The other night I was hurrying to eat so I could go shopping with my sister. My Dad was watching and said 'That's awfully big bites, young lady.' I started eating tiny bites in a very prim way and he got mad. When my mother asked me what was wrong, I told her I was sick of Dad being the 'eating supervisor.' She said I was being disrespectful and that the conversation was over."

In another family, the mother was extremely nutrition conscious. Her daughter commented, "I always have to eat at meals whether I am hungry or not. I must have at least three glasses of milk a day. If I told my mother I had just binged, she would want to know what I ate and if it was nutritious."

The therapist must enlist the parent's aid in removing pressure about food. They must be encouraged to avoid commenting on amounts of food eaten, when it is eaten, how it is eaten. The therapist must state that he/she is aware how difficult this may be at times. Parents often ask "How am I to deal with it when I find a half of gallon of ice cream missing. I don't want my other children to eat it. How do I explain to them that Mary can have it but they can't. . . It just isn't right."

This emphasis on what is "right" will come up repeatedly in family therapy sessions and is an integral part of the problem. These parents often have very rigidly defined standards of what is "right." The waste of food that occurs with bulimia is offensive and "just not right." Frequently a history of struggle exists between the parents and the child around food consumption. Sometimes a pattern develops of parents buying food and hiding it so that the child won't consume it and waste it. This can result in a pathological game of parents hiding food and the daughter searching the house, finding the food, and binging on it. Parents may even go to the extreme of locking cupboards and refrigerator in an attempt to control the child's eating.

At the same time that the parents are trying to control the food, the child is learning to become increasingly secretive in her consumption. She may go to great lengths to hide evidence of her food habits, such as disposing of food wrappers and laxative packages so that they won't be found. She also will attempt to avoid detection of vomiting activities. One client, Ruth, described, "My parents would ask me frequently if I was still doing 'it.' The 'it' was throwing up. I didn't want to get them mad or upset so I lied and said 'no.' What I really was doing was going down to the basement and throwing up into a paper bag and throwing it behind the furnace. You can imagine the mess when they found this after it had been going on a year. Even then they just yelled at me and told me to 'stop it.' Nobody thought that I might need counseling. I was only eleven so I didn't know either."

Ruth's experience illustrates the remarkable denial of a problem that can occur in some of these families. Ruth's parents not only ignored the purging behavior but also failed to seek professional help when their daughter lost weight until she weighed only 67 pounds. Not until Ruth was in college and had struggled with bulimia for over ten years did she seek counseling on her own. Even then, she had difficulty in making a commitment to therapy because of the stigma that her family had communicated to her regarding getting outside help.

Obviously, the kind of power struggle that develops between the parent and the child over food is fueling the binge/purge behavior. In many of the enmeshed families, the structure is so rigid that food consumption is one of the few ways the adolescent is able to rebel against parental authority and to feel some internal control. Although the parents may be resistant to the idea of relinquishing their efforts to control the food, doing so is vital to the recovery process. The therapist must insist that they stop all comments about their daughter's eating and all attempts to control her food intake. The therapist may need to point out that, "What you are doing isn't working. Maybe it is time to try another approach."

Is the Responsibility Which Is Placed on or Assumed by the Client Discussed Openly in Family Therapy?

As described previously, the daughter that develops bulimia is often in the role of responsible child in the family. The therapist must make a concerted effort to remove her from this position. This means helping the family restructure itself in a more appropriate pattern. This may be difficult and be met with resistance. After all, having the daughter who has bulimia always present to take over other's responsibilities may be a real advantage to which parents and other family members have become accustomed.

Sometimes the family is already aware of the problem. Sharon's father commented, "Nobody in this family is allowed to argue with anybody else. As soon as a disagreement starts, Sharon is right there in the middle of it. She can't stand to see anyone angry so nothing ever gets settled. I tell her it is normal for families to fight once in a while but she won't stand any of it." Sharon agreed with his statement and added that, "I can't stand to have anyone angry with me. I always apologize to the other person even if I know I am right. I guess I always thought everybody felt as bad as I do when someone is mad at them. That's why I always try to stop the fights."

If one or both parents have been contributing to the feelings of responsibility by using the daughter as a confidant, this behavior must be discouraged. This was especially true in the case of Sharon and her mother. In family therapy, Sharon was able to express her distress at being told too much about her mother's concerns. "What happens when you tell me these things is that I feel like I should fix them. I really can't do that so what I do is try to become more perfect myself so I won't be another item on your worry list." Sharon's mother countered by saying that they had always prided themselves on being an "open" family and that "Now I won't know how to talk to Sharon. I won't feel comfortable about saying anything to her. I feel like we have to watch every word we say." Sharon was asked to help her mother by listing the areas about which she becomes most uncomfortable when told. She stated, "I don't want to hear about your marital problems, family financial problems, or your worries about my brothers and sisters. I can't do anything about these issues and it just upsets me to hear about them." Sharon's mother agreed to try to avoid these topics.

In Gina's family, she was often drawn into the disputes between her mother and father. Her mother had been threatening to initiate divorce proceedings against her father for years. She always tied her taking action to something happening in Gina's life. For example, the father was a carpenter who did much of the work on building a home for Gina and her husband. Gina was told, "As soon as your father finishes working on your house, I'm going to start on the divorce." When Gina told her mother she would be going into the hospital to get treatment for her bulimia, her mother said, "As soon as you get over this eating thing, I probably will go ahead with the divorce." Gina finally worked up the courage to tell her mother to stop making her responsible for the breakup or continuation of the marriage. Her mother was amazed when Gina pointed out the many times she had tied the divorce decision to something happening in her daughter's life.

Is One Sibling Sometimes Placed in the Responsible Role by Other Siblings?

Sometimes the siblings have an investment in keeping the individual in the responsible child role. In Sharon's family, a younger sister had been born seven years after the other siblings. The father commented, "We never have been able to discipline Tina properly. Whenever she did something wrong her brothers and sisters were there to cover-up for her or to get in between if there was a confrontation." At the time of family therapy, Sharon was the only one of the older siblings still living at home. Tina used Sharon's fear of her father's temper to keep her running interference for her. Through therapy, Sharon saw how Tina was using her but was unable to resist Tina's manipulation. In the end, the only solution was for Sharon to move out of the house and into her own apartment. Even then, Sharon stated, "I feel like I have abandoned Tina and Mom. I will feel terrible if anything happens to either one of them."

When the Symptomatic Child Leaves the Family, Does Another Family Member Develop a Problem?

An interesting point to note is that when the symptomatic child, who in these families is the child with bulimia, recovers or is removed from the family by hospitalization or moving out, often another family member develops a problem. The family seems to need a problem on which to focus which often helps to avoid marital conflict between the parents. For example, when Janet started recovering from her bulimia, her sister started openly defying the parents and staying out all night. When Sharon entered a hospital eating disorders unit, her sister began drinking and skipping school. The mother in this family also began having panic attacks and was unable to function. The therapist will need to be aware of the possibility of this happening and help the client with bulimia not feel responsible. She will have a strong urge to "make everything all right again."

Will the Therapist Assist with Communication Problems Among Family Members?

One of the biggest complaints of teenagers with bulimia who are living at home is that "My mother (father) never listens to me." For example, Kathy stated, "When I tell my mother that I really hate school, the only answer I get is, 'You will just have to get over it.' My parents have the belief that anybody can overcome anything if you 'just pull yourself up by your bootstraps.' They never even ask why I hate school.'"

Carrie described her interaction with her mother, "I went to try to talk to my mother about something that was really bothering me. In the middle of my trying to tell her, she launched into this big lecture about how bad it is to take drugs and drink. It really didn't have anything to do with what I was saying. It felt like I had pushed a button and a tape recorder had come on with a pre-recorded message about drinking and drugs." Carrie went on to say, "The day school started, she asked me how things went. I told her several things I had liked but then I said that I wasn't sure I would like my English teacher. I immediately got the tape recording about how I don't realize how lucky I am and how much harder things were when she went to school. I feel like I can't talk to her about anything without getting one of her lectures which may not even be on the same subject. Why can't she just listen?"

In the family session it was clear what Carrie meant. On several occasions, the mother launched into one of her lectures, using a very authoritative tone of voice and pointing a finger at Carrie for emphasis. The therapist stopped her and asked, "Do you hear what you are doing right now? What message do you think your daughter is getting? What is it you are really trying to communicate?" At other times, the mother was asked to repeat in her own words what she heard her daughter say. It gradually became clear to mother that she wasn't listening. At the same time the therapist was making these interventions, the therapist also commented on how hard the mother was trying and how very important it was to her that her children turned out right. The therapist made it clear that she supported the mother's intention to help but pointed out that the way she was going about it was likely to backfire. "When a parent reacts to big issues and little issues with strong feelings and equal emphasis, pretty soon the teenager learns to tune out everything the person says. If she feels like you are not really listening, she gradually will stop talking to you completely. A much better approach is to listen and keep the lines of communication open and save your influence for the really big issues. You have done a very good job of raising a daughter with high moral standards and goals. It really is all right to relax a little."

**Listening and Acting,
Can the Therapist Help?**

While the therapist is teaching listening skills, he/she will emphasize to both parents and children that the individual telling about an issue does not necessarily expect action from the listener. Both the parents and their daughter are likely to have a pattern of immediately launching into problem solving or a rescue mission to relieve the talker of the problem. Many times, just feeling like they are being heard and understood is the most important factor. Often, relieving the listener of the pressure to *do something* allows the teller to pay more attention to what is actually being said.

**How Can Parents Learn to
Give Praise More Effectively?**

At the same time that the therapist is teaching listening skills, attention will need to be given to the means by which approval or praise is given to the child by the parents. This can most effectively be done in a session when the child is not present. Then, when the parents change their pattern of giving praise, the daughter does not credit it to the therapist. The kind of comment the therapist might make to the parents is, "I know that praise and approval is frequently expressed in your family. I'm wondering if you've ever thought about the way praise is given. One way commonly used by parents is to say, 'That's really nice, dear, I'm so proud of you.' That sounds fine, doesn't it? Let's consider another way. 'That's really nice dear, you must be so proud of yourself.' Do you feel the difference? Your daughter has very little in the way of internal self-approval. She is almost totally dependent on the input of others to determine how she feels about herself. Changing the way you give praise can really help her start to develop important feelings of self-worth. Practice saying things like 'You must be pleased with the way that you handled that problem,' and 'It must feel good to have accomplished that.' You will be communicating your approval but even more important you will be building her own sense of worth."

**Summary Comments on
Communication Skills**

Obviously, what the therapist is teaching are basic communication skills. What was covered here is only a brief outline of teaching attentive listening and giving praise. If the therapist or client wishes to pursue this further, several fine books are available including: *Parent Effectiveness Training* by Gordon and McKay (1970).

SPOUSE/PARTNER RELATIONSHIP ISSUES
MARITAL THERAPY

Some of the clients seen for bulimia will be married or living with a partner. Although, for the ease of expression, we refer to the partner as a husband or spouse, the material covered here is equally applicable to non-married partners.

How Do Couples Relate
When She Has Bulimia?

It is interesting to note the variety of ways in which the couples choose to deal with the bulimia. In some of the relationships, the bulimia is carefully concealed from the spouse, sometimes for years. With others, the partner is aware of the binge/purge behavior before marriage but may have the hope that it will go away after the marriage occurs. The reaction of the spouse to the bulimia varies greatly. Some of the partners ignore the behavior and rarely comment on it. Others actively disapprove of the bulimia and may resort to harassment and ridicule. Some may vacillate between these two positions. A smaller number seem actively to sabotage the woman's efforts to recover. This sabotage is often based on the fear that the woman will leave the marriage if she recovers. Most partners are willing to participate in counseling if it will help but regard the bulimia as "her problem."

Many of the partners have attempted to help their spouse control the eating behavior. This is often frustrating and is rarely effective. The client is often ashamed of her behavior and will avoid communicating with the partner about the subject.

How Can the Partner Help?

One of the major goals of marital counseling is to teach the client how to clearly express what she needs from her partner. He will need specific instructions as to which of his efforts are helpful and which are counter-productive. The needs expressed by the client vary widely and cannot be clearly predicted by the therapist. A very important aspect is to help her decide what suits her needs. For example, one woman said it helped when she was trying to keep down a meal if her partner would gently massage her stomach and talk quietly with her. Another stated that the last thing she wanted was any touching especially of her abdomen when she was feeling fat after eating. Any affection or physical contact at that point would considerably heighten her desire to purge. Instead, she needed to be allowed to sit quietly and listen to music or her relaxation tape until the "fat feeling" passed.

Other clients have suggested a variety of ways the spouse could help. Sometimes having him take over the meal preparation for a while helps. With other women, the most difficult period may be cleaning and putting away food at the end of the meal. Sometimes, the help involves other issues unrelated to food. One client really needed her husband's support and encouragement to quit a job that paid well but was highly stressful and competitive. Another asked her partner to be more attentive to her when visiting his relatives. She felt abandoned when he wandered off with his cousins and left her alone with his sister and mother.

The woman may well have taken on a similar role in her marriage to that which she had in her family of origin. She is likely to do a great deal of "mind reading" to anticipate her partner's needs or desires. She often is very unassertive about her own needs and will avoid open conflict. These issues will need to be discussed in sessions with the partner.

Can the Therapist Help the Partner Understand the Bigger Problem—Emotional Issues?

The partner must be helped to understand that bulimia is not exclusively a food problem. When some of the underlying emotional issues are explained to him, he is often considerably more supportive and understanding. Frequently when the issues are openly discussed and he has had an opportunity to ask questions, he gains considerable relief.

Do the Client, Partner, and Children Meet in Marital Therapy?

Sometimes children are present in the client's family. Gloria had two step-children from her husband's previous marriage. As she explains it, "I am very jealous of the two kids. When they are at our house and I am at work, I fantasize that they are eating my food. I hate it when Bob brings home bags of junk food just before they visit. The youngest, Carol, is developing quite a weight problem and the kids are making fun of her at school. Everytime I see her I remember when I was the fat kid at school and I feel all those old feelings. I'm really confused about my feelings towards the kids and I'm afraid that soon it will really hurt my marriage."

Clearly some family sessions including the step-children were necessary for Gloria and Bob. Initially, Bob was very protective of his children and refused to involved them in counseling. As Gloria struggled to recover from the bulimia, gradually Bob understood that her feelings toward the children were hindering the recovery and he reluctantly consented to involve them. Several sessions took place which resulted in a much more comfortable relationship between Gloria and the children which was followed by further improvement in her eating behavior.

Sarah had two teenage children that were unaware of her binge/purge behavior. Her oldest daughter, Jane, was aware of her mother's frequent attempts to lose weight and was critical of her size. If she encountered her mother when she was eating, Jane frequently made critical comments such as, "Are you eating again?" "Should you be eating that?" These criticisms were similar to those made to Sarah by her father when she was growing up and had the effect of increasing her feelings of deprivation and worthlessness. Sarah responded by gorging and later feeling guilty and hopeless.

In a family session, Sarah's problems with bulimia were explained to her daughter. Jane understood how her comments were causing negative reactions and became much more supportive and encouraging toward her mother.

SUMMARY

In summary, dealing with the families of women with bulimia is an important part of the recovery process. Family issues will need to be addressed in therapy whether or not the family members are available for sessions. If the client is young and still living with her parents, involving them and sometimes the siblings is usually necessary and can be quite helpful. The concept of the Irregular Person can lead to some understanding of the destructive relationships many of these women have with their parents. If the client is married or in a committed relationship, involving the partner and possibly their children can be helpful.

CHAPTER **12**

RECOVERY ISSUES

The client with bulimia is often impatient to recover. The personality traits of perfectionism and need for approval often drive her desire to recover and put this part of her life behind her. The client must feel better about herself and be able to develop coping skills before the binge eating will cease. As the person develops increased self esteem and ego strength, she begins to use the other coping skills rather than binges to deal with stress. As the client begins to use eating less frequently as a solution to stress, she starts to see herself as "cured." An important measure is that the therapist should not terminate seeing these clients prematurely. Often the bulimia returns with increased intensity just as the client declares herself to be recovered.

After the binge/purge behavior has diminished or ceased, counseling likely will be necessary to improve other areas of functioning such as relationship issues, sexual functioning, and career decisions. In this section we will discuss several issues that commonly arise during the recovery from the binge eating behavior. The specific issues that will be presented are dealing with the awareness that the behavior isn't working any more, taking responsibility for the quantity of food consumed, and learning to cope with relapses.

What Constitutes Recovery?

A definition of what constitutes recovery in the client with bulimia is difficult to state. Some authors use the reduction or cessation of binge/purge behavior as indicative of cure. Our feelings are that cessation of the binges is a significant part of the criterion for recovery, however, while this is a major goal, it cannot be considered the entire definition of success. To approach the treatment of bulimia by prescription of anti-depressive medication and calling the patient "cured" because of reduction or cessation of binges is analogous to early claims of success in the treatment of anorexia by body weight restoration. The identifying symptom may have been altered, but the psychological distress that caused the symptom is still present.

**What Happens When the
Binges Stop Working?**

At some point in the recovery process, the client will come to the realization that the bulimic behavior isn't "working" any longer. "I am still binging, but I don't really know why. I don't get the same feelings of relief that I used to get when I binge and purge." This realization may produce some anxiety in the woman as she becomes aware that her long relied upon coping skills are no longer helping. When this issue is explored, she often realizes that the intensity of the binging is changing also. "I am not eating as much as I used to when I binge. I stop sooner because I just don't feel like continuing to eat. I used to have these 'mega binges' where I would eat and throw up for several cycles but these have just about stopped completely. What I'm doing now feels more like a habit than anything else." Many clients seem to share this perception that they have two kinds of binges and that the feelings involved with each are somewhat different. What we have come to call "mega binges" are driven by intense feelings of guilt, anger, depression, and inadequacy. The binge session may go on for several hours punctuated by vomiting to enable the consumption of more food. The other type of binge that seems to appear as recovery proceeds is more of a "habit binge." This binging behavior has less intense feelings associated with it such as boredom and frustration. The amount consumed is considerably smaller. The individual may be surprised to find herself stopping before she consumes all the food she has prepared.

What Other Emotions Arise as the Binging Behavior Becomes Less Effective?

The loss of effectiveness of the binge behavior is greeted with mixed emotions by the client. She recognizes this as a positive sign of recovery, but at the same time, is slightly panicked by the loss of the ability to blot out feelings with food. In some clients, loss of effectiveness of the binges causes an increase in anxiety which in turn promotes an increase in binge behavior with the hope of re-establishing its effectiveness as a coping skill. This last ditch stand of the symptom may cause the client to become discouraged and feel as though her progress has been lost. This is rarely the case. The renewed intensity of the binging seems to fade out fairly quickly and the client then returns to the improved level of functioning.

How Does Recovery Affect the Need to Eat?

The woman will become aware that she is making more choices about food. For example, Gina commented, "We were out at one of my favorite fast food places and I didn't really feel hungry. I found myself ordering just a baked potato with cheese instead of a full meal. In the past, I never would have noticed if I was hungry, I would have eaten everything and thrown it up." Lisa stated, "I am finding myself standing in front of the refrigerator asking myself what it is I feel like eating instead of consuming everything in sight. Sometimes I realize that it isn't food I want at all. I'm getting better at discriminating real hunger from emotional hunger."

Can Retaining Food in the
Stomach Become a Problem
During Recovery?

As the woman begins to make efforts to reduce binge/purge activity, she sometimes becomes aware that retaining food in her stomach is difficult. The frequent reversal of the normal forward motion of the stomach can result in a delay of stomach emptying. The individual may have difficulty tolerating the feeling of food in her stomach for prolonged periods. This problem and its treatment is discussed in the chapter on "medical aspects of bulimia." The woman may want to experiment with eating several small meals a day to avoid feeling full.

As Recovery Progresses, How
Can Use of Other Coping Skills
Be Encouraged?

"I choose to binge." The recovery stage requires some active intervention on the part of the therapist to encourage strongly the client to try other ways of coping with stress. One of the ways that can give the client time to think before diving into the food is to require them to perform a task before they binge. For example, the therapist might say "From now on, whenever you are about to binge, I want you to write out the sentence 'I choose to binge.' After that, you can go on to binge if you need to. You do not need to bring me the sentences or even count them for me. What I do want you to is to notice how you are feeling when you write the sentence. What is going on in your life that is causing the drive to binge to build up?"

Clients often do not like this assignment. They may actively resist accepting responsibility for the binge behavior. The therapist needs to inform the client that binges do not just happen. No dark and mysterious force decends over them and leads them to food. Acceptance that binging is a choice is important to recovery. This exercise should not be used until the client is showing signs of being ready to give up binging. To make the assignment too early in treatment often results in feelings of failure and hopelessness.

A wide variety of responses have been made concerning this assignment. Some report no effect at all, but others have very intense reactions. Cindy stated, "I wrote the sentence down, looked at, and changed it to 'I choose not to binge.' Then I burst into tears. I realized that I was upset at a grade I got on a paper. After I cried a while I decided I didn't need the binge after all." Lynn could not make herself write the sentence until after the binge when she wrote, "I chose to binge." Some cannot force themselves to write it at all. Karen reported, "I really did not want to admit I was making the choice. I felt very angry whenever I went to write it down." Sharon jokingly told the group, "I spelled it out in chocolate chip cookies and then ate it!" Regardless of the reaction, this assignment provides rich material for therapy sessions.

Another helpful method is to have the client make a list of alternate coping skills and post them in a prominent place. This technique is helpful because, when the drive to binge is building, the woman may have difficulty thinking of anything else. This can be a list of activities such as jogging, calling a friend, and so forth or it can be what one client called her "prescription to pull myself out of a slump." Her prescription included: stop eating sweets, force myself to continue social activities even if I am feeling fat, avoid self-pity and blaming, eat whenever I am hungry but only when I am hungry, and don't stay home from work.

How Do Women with Bulimia Learn to Control the Amount of Food They Eat?

One of the difficulties faced during recovery is having to give up being able to eat enormous amounts of food. Some of the women reported that they get considerable pleasure out of eating large quantities of food and that they are reluctant to give up this habit. With others, little pleasure is taken in the taste of the food, however, almost all have the fear that "I will have to exist on next to nothing if I give up purging." This fear can be addressed by dietary counseling as discussed in the chapter on nutrition. The client also may also have to give up ever reaching her goal weight which is generally inappropriately low for her height and body build. This acceptance is easier as self-worth becomes intrinsic to the individual, rather than solely defined by others or society.

Do Relapses Occur?

Relapses are frequent in the recovery stage. This may partly be due to the pressure the women puts on herself. As Lynn put it, "Once I started controlling the behavior once in a while, I felt like I had to control it all the time. I felt guilty when I failed and this lead to the next binge." Lynn was informed that she was again striving to be perfect and was attempting to control her bulimia by force. Just as if she were gripping a handful of sand too tightly, she was losing control by hanging on with too much force.

The pressure the woman puts on herself to be fully recovered may cause her to avoid reaching out to her therapist or other group members. Cindy reported, "Once I told you I had been controlling my eating, I was afraid to tell you I was having trouble. I didn't want to let you down. Finally, it got so bad, I binged."

Another reason frequent relapses occur is that, as the woman begins to feel she no longer has bulimia, she pressures herself to do all the things she told herself she couldn't do before. As Cathy explained, "Now that I was no longer binging, I felt like I had to make all the decisions I had put off until I got rid of my eating problems. My career, my relationship with my boyfriend, my entire future had to be determined *right now*. I panicked and started binging again."

For some, the self-destructive pattern has extended for so long that they are afraid to let go of it. The bulimia and the emotional turmoil associated with it appears to have become part of their identity. This fear was expressed vividly by Cindy, "If I let go of the pain and make that change, will I be who I am still? I'm scared. I come up to a point of being almost there and I blow it. That's what I am doing now. I am touching palm to palm with who I am and I am running away."

**Do Significant Others
Sometimes Interfere
with Recovery?**

For some, significant people in their lives may sabotage the recovery process. Amy had the bulimia before she married. Her husband, George had developed a significant alcohol problem while on active duty in Viet Nam. When they had disagreements, George would be critical of Amy's eating and her weight; Amy would accuse George of being an alcoholic. When Amy began making progress on reducing her binge behavior, she would begin to find food hidden around the house, usually in places that she would be likely to find it. If she successfully avoided consuming this food, George would bring a chocolate cake, one of Amy's favorite binge foods, home from the bakery and leave it on the kitchen counter. When Amy started attending evening group therapy sessions, she invariably would come home to find George passed out on the couch. George denied any attempt at sabotage, refused to acknowledge his drinking problem, and refused to come with Amy for marriage counseling.

Another woman, Sally, realized "I am afraid to get healthy. The only time my mother pays attention to me is when I am sick. Each time I have to get sicker or more depressed to get her to notice. I see the pattern now but part of me wants to keep trying to get her attention. I will have to give that up if I give up the bulimia."

Is Prescribing a Relapse an Effective Technique?

One way the therapist helps the client avoid the relapse problem is to prescribe it. Like prescribing the symptom mentioned earlier, prescribing a relapse helps relieve the guilt if a relapse does happen. The therapist might say something like, "This all seems almost too good to be true. I wonder if you are really ready for all this progress. You may need a relapse before you get any better." If the relapse does not occur, the client can be delighted to prove the therapist wrong. If it does occur, the impact on the client has been minimized, and telling the therapist about the relapse will be easier for her. After all, the relapse was expected and even recommended!

Will the Binge-Purge Episode Ever be Seen as an Individual Event?

A major step in the recovery process seems to occur when the woman can see a binge-purge episode as an individual event rather than "the first in a never ending series for the rest of my life." This cognitive shift seems to reduce some of the pressure and the guilt surrounding binging. She needs to be told that, "Binge eating will be on your list of ways of coping with stress for the rest of your life. Hopefully, you will have many other things on that list that you can use so that you rarely get to the point of binging. In the future, if you find yourself turning to food to solve your problems, use that as a sign to examine your life and determine either what you need to be doing to help yourself or what you need to stop doing to reduce your stress."

With Recovery Will Views of "Normal" People and Self Change?

Women with bulimia often have an idealized view of how "normal" people go through life. In groups or in individual sessions, questions are often asked of the therapist as to how "normal" people would respond to certain situations. To the client with bulimia, normal people are never moody or depressed. They never doubt themselves or worry about their weight. They would never be troubled by relationships with parents or have sexual problems. In the final phases of therapy, an important step is to check out the standard to which the client is comparing herself to judge her recovery. Remember, these women have accepted a great deal of the media presentation of the "perfect" self. They are surprised to know that "normal" people have a variety of problems but that the main difference between those needing therapy and those not needing therapy is how they deal with the problems of life.

As Recovery Progresses, Will the Time Span Between Sessions Increase?

When the client appears to be reaching the point that therapy is no longer necessary, a wise decision is to space out the sessions to every other week and then once a month. Even when the client is no longer having periodic sessions, she should be reassured that the door is open for future sessions if they should become necessary. A common occurence is for the client to come back for a few supportive sessions six months to a year after terminating regular periodic therapy.

Termination of a client's regular therapy sessions is both a happy and sad time for both the client and the therapist. As a team, they have often worked together for an extended period of time. The issues they have confronted have been intense and emotional. Frequently the bonds of friendship and caring have developed to the point where separation is approached reluctantly by both. Often the client maintains contact with group members and the therapist for an extended period of time throughout life. A pleasant event always occurs when receiving a note in the mail telling of marriage, a new job, graduate school completion, a new baby, and other significant life events. Watching these women grow and thrive as the burden of bulimia is left behind is always a joy.

One of the women expressed her feelings as she terminated therapy in a poem:

The Dawn Came

And the dawn came
And it was warm
The little girl felt a loosening
Of her mother's hand
She turned as a leaf
Moving with the breeze
Yet firmly rooted to the ground
Warmness seeped through her shirt,
Through her trembling body,
Nurturing, strengthening,
Stilling the areas that had been
Crying and shaking
While she sat for so long, alone,
In the chill of the cold night.
And the woman in her gently
Removed her mother's hand.
She ventured forth
Towards the crest of the hill
And as she walked,
She felt a newness, a glowing.
Her garden had grown and
It lay before her,
Merging into the rolling hills
Which seemed to stretch forever,
Each blade, each tree stood,
In quiet clarity,
In the dawn.

SUMMARY

In summary, several issues typically are confronted in the recovery stage of treatment for bulimia. Reactions to changes in behavior and attitudes toward food will need to be attended to. The client will need help dealing with new demands she places upon herself now that she has "recovered." A plan for coping with relapses will need to be developed. The client's definition of normal will have to be adjusted to more closely fit reality. Gradual discontinuation of therapy sessions with permission for follow-up sessions should be arranged.

MARGARET ALBERI FLYNN

Margaret Alberi Flynn, Ph.D., R.D., is a professor in Family and Community Medicine in the School of Medicine, University of Missouri, Columbia, Missouri. She teaches college and medical students, has published 35 research papers, and is involved in patient care.

CHAPTER 13

NUTRITION, HEALTH, AND THE DIETITIAN

Margaret A. Flynn, Ph.D., R.D.

Eating plays a highly significant role in the quality and quantity of our lives. We have particular attitudes toward food which influence our behavior toward its use. Sometimes a particular combination of personality features and life events results in an individual developing an eating disorder.

The authors wish to thank Cynthia Palmer, R.D., Deaconess Hospital, St. Louis, for her assistance in editing this chapter.

Does Food Serve Social and Emotional Needs as Well as Nutritional?

Our individual responses toward food are entwined in our interrelationships with the rules of our peer group, society, and our culture. For example, each sub-group in the larger culture has its own traditional avenues involving food acquisition, preparation, and when, where, and how the food is eaten. For most people, food is not just nutrition. Due to cultural learning experiences it has come to meet a number of emotional and social needs. Friendship and eating go together; almost all social encounters are organized around eating and drinking. Food is exchanged as a gift offering to demonstrate affection or gratefulness, such as "nothing says lovin' like something from the oven," or "if you really love mother, you'll clean your plate." Holiday gatherings related to food take on a significance well beyond just nutrition to stay alive. Food taboos can even take on great social significance when two groups with conflicting rules meet. For the Hindus in India, the eating of cows is taboo and the eating of pork taboo for the Muslims. These differences in food preferences between Hindus and Muslims in pre-partitioned India caused disagreements and occasional outbreaks of violence.

Where Do We Obtain Our Attitudes About Food?

The feelings, attitudes, and rituals that people have about foods are learned over the long period of time that infants and children are dependent on others for food. For babies, food and feeding are comfort, love, and affection. For every newborn, emotions become attached to feedings which affect their eating patterns later in life. All of us have special food memories, some pleasant, some less so. During this time most of us learn some food taboos, which we cannot overcome even under the best of conditions. For example, few in our culture consider dogs or horses edible. At early developmental stages eating can become a substitute for care, love, and relief of frustrations. Depending on how the care giver reacts, food can be withheld as punishment or given as a reward. When the child can want, demand, and receive satisfactory food, he/she has learned to control him/herself and manipulate others.

Do Different Foods
Satisfy Our Emotional Needs?

Food may become a "bridge over troubled waters" for adults when used as an outlet or crutch for dealing with frustration, anxiety, despondency, boredom, disappointment, and loneliness. Emotional stress may change the way we eat; for example, we may find ourselves eating more high energy foods or eating between meals. Food also can be a source of sensory pleasure. In dealing with food all of our senses can be involved: the smell and taste of food may reactivate long forgotten memories, the color and texture of food can create a pleasant feeling much like viewing a great work of art, and even the sounds food makes while cooking can stir emotions within us.

Our Western habit is to eat three meals a day, but even something done this frequently seldom becomes purely habitual. We make decisions about what to eat based on our emotional well-being as well as on our physical needs. Some very strong emotions may be behind our decisions of what and when to eat. Food eaten in a situation where the emotional support was deeply felt, e.g., Thanksgiving dinners with grandparents and other relatives, may take on a number of positive meanings for the individual; whereas, the same foods, if eaten repetitively because the family was poor, may take on negative connotations.

CHANGING EATING PATTERNS

What Motivational Changes
Affect Eating Patterns?

As we mature, our motivations concerning food change. We may be motivated to become a part of a social group which has special food tastes, such as lobster, oysters, and squid. Or we may join a group that practices a more restricted diet than we are used to, such as that followed by vegetarians. A common motivation for changing eating habits is related to the desire for a new body image. A wide range of unusual diets which call for major changes in foods eaten and the pattern in which they are eaten exist to meet this demand for a slimmer body.

Do Eating Habits
Become Compelling Issues?

Sometimes when changes in our eating habits become an issue, emotional overtones may show up. Stress can be created when we are forced to confront our feelings about food and eating. Guilt feelings can arise when a food that signifies conflicting values to the eater is ingested. Jews, Muslims, Seventh Day Adventists, and others prohibit the eating of pork. If a person who belongs to one of these groups attends a picnic where barbequed pork ribs are the tradition, internal conflict may be present. A fat person who eats sweets to excess may be conflicted because he/she knows that this is "junk food." However, this junk food also may represent a comfort because it serves as a substitute for a lack of affection or attention in his/her life. This use of food as a temporary antidepressant may be followed by feelings of despondency because of a lack of control.

Can Failure with Dieting
Be the Start of Bulimia?

Whether a person goes on a diet for health reasons or just for cosmetic reasons, that person is likely to approach dieting with high expectations as to results. If that person is successful, he/she will experience a feeling of euphoria. On the other hand, if the diet fails for any reason, the individual may feel depressed. Diets often involve a major change of eating patterns, use of unusual foods and chronic feelings of hunger. Because most diets cause discomfort from deprivation, the dieter may vow to avoid the travail of attempting to lose weight. The bulimia may serve as an alternative to this discomfort from deprivation.

ADOLESCENT EATING PATTERNS

Understanding the lifestyle and eating behavior of adolescents will help us gain a better appreciation of how eating disorders have come to be an accepted way of life among some young women. Story (1984) stated: "Biological, psychosocial, cognitive, social, and developmental changes have a dynamic effect on the eating behavior of adolescents. The adolescent's search for independence and identity, active lifestyle, and concern for appearance may result in missed meals, eating away from home, increased snacking, and adoption of fad diets and nontraditional eating patterns" (p. 77).

What Family Characteristics
Affect Eating Patterns of
Adolescents?

Up to a certain age the family unit is the major influence on an adolescent's food habits, values, and attitudes. At some point, values external to the family begin to be felt. When the family structure is unusual or extreme, i.e., overly rigid or permissive, the adolescents will be apt to use food and eating behavior to demonstrate anger and rebellion. They may do this by going on bizarre food binges, refusing to eat certain foods traditionally eaten by the family, going on fasts, or simply skipping the families regularly planned meals. Love and Johnson (1985) list the characteristics of families who have an individual with bulimia as "disengaged, chaotic, highly conflictal, deficient in problem solving skills, and, while they value achievement they provide little support of intellectual pursuits" (p. 5).

Today in many families both parents work and in single parent families the custodial parent often must work outside the home. When working parents do not have time to prepare regular meals, negative effects may occur on the family members' eating habits. Teenagers who are expected to fend for food on their own may develop weird eating habits as a result of this freedom. Just as their dress code, language, and dating behavior are influenced by peers, their eating behavior also may become centered around peer's food and drink preferences. Overweight adolescents who feel isolated from a peer group may attempt bizarre weight loss methods in order to gain acceptance.

Has Mass Media Affected
the Eating and Drinking
Patterns?

Additional influence on the eating and drinking habits of adolescents comes from the mass media. Story (1984) pointed out that the purpose of advertising is to entice, make an impression, and grab attention in order to persuade consumers to buy. To do this, the advertisers prey on fears of adolescents of not being attractive or popular with others. They offer their product as the royal road to social acceptance. A common feature of these ads are pictures of thin women and athletic men; these advertisements support an ideal body image which often is unrealistic and unobtainable yet is much sought after by teenagers.

Story (1984) elucidated the problems well:

"Life style behaviors that foster poor eating habits are also repeatedly portrayed on television. People in successful occupations are shown as eating-on-the-run or being too busy to eat nutritiously. Commercials encourage snacking between meals, usually on high calorie, low nutrient snacks. These advertisements are frequently filled with attractive, healthy-looking slender people living energetic lives. The commercials thus present a dichotomous situation in which individuals are able to remain thin and full of energy and yet have eating habits that may be counter to this" (p. 82).

Alternative lifestyles and fad diets seem especially attractive to teenagers who are living in families that have much conflict among members. These adolescents are searching for their identity and independence. In this search, their physical appearance, especially their weight, becomes a driving force in their lives. Knowing this, the ad writers play on teenagers' hopes that they too can achieve an ideal thinness if they will only use this method of weight loss, this diet supplement, or this diet pill. These "pitches" are often too sophisticated for the adolescent who does not have the background to distinguish between actuality and fabrication. Even a knowledgeable adolescent can become very confused between knowing and doing what is healthy versus doing what looks good. The short term but immediate gains in attractiveness may outweigh the long term health benefits.

One must keep in mind, however, that diet patterns need not be those generally accepted as "normal" to be nutritionally adequate. Atypical eating patterns may have a sound basis. A vegetarian diet or a diet based only on fast food may be quite sufficient for good health. Our point is that an eating pattern needs to be carefully evaluated to see if it actually is a health risk.

Do Adolescents Eating
Habits Affect Nutrition?

Adolescents, young independent workers, and professionals consume more of their meals and snacks outside the home. Fast-food restaurants are extremely popular adolescent gathering places; they hire teenagers who help serve the kind of food that has a special appeal. While fast foods can be part of a nutritious diet, dependence upon them may herald various nutritional problems. To properly evaluate the diet, one needs to pay attention to how often fast foods are eaten, the nutritional value of other foods also eaten, and the dietary needs of the individual involved. Common deficiencies include iron, calcium, vitamin C, folic acid, and low fiber content. Common excesses include high sodium and fat content. When adolescents engage in outside-of-school activities or work for extra money, this can result in impulsive or irregular eating habits. Teenage girls who omit breakfast or lunch in order to "save calories," may compensate by the consumption of a large amount of food at one time. This type of eating could precipitate the beginning of a learned pattern leading to bulimia.

DIETITIAN'S ROLE IN TEAM TREATMENT

Who Will Be Members of the Team?

Treatment will vary with each individual but the treatment of women who have bulimia should be a team effort. Members of a team most likely to cover all aspects of care for clients with bulimia are a combination of three professional members—a psychologist, a physician, and a clinical dietitian—and the client. Each of these professionals should be aware of the skills of the other team members and respect one another's unique contribution to the client's welfare. Clients may find that their particular needs are best met by one specific member of the team and choose to work more closely with that person, or the client may find all three contributing in a significant way to her progress.

Why a Clinical Dietitian?

The dietary counseling should be done by a clinical dietitian who has graduated from an accredited dietetics program and who is registered as a clinical dietitian. In preparation to deal with these problems the clinical dietitian will have had courses that relate physiological, psychological, and dietary factors to one another.

Is the Treatment Program Individualized?

One of the challenges of developing a treatment program for some-one with bulimia is in individualization of the treatment plan. A program based on the client's personality and history is more likely to lead to a gradual decrease in binge eating, vomiting, and purging. Concomitant with this decrease should be a decrease in the amount of time the client spends preoccupied with thoughts about food and eating. As part of the treatment program, each client is expected to become a part of the treatment team. As part of the team she helps to set goals and is expected to seek information, advice and support from her treatment triad.

What Are Some Long Term Goals?

The long term goals of treatment are to help the client regain control over her eating and to develop appropriate and healthy eating patterns. Straight forward discussions are held regarding the fact that bulimic behavior will not stop immediately and she is likely to have relapses. Slow progress is to be expected. She also is helped to recognize that many of the obsessive attitudes about food, eating, body weight, and body shape which precipitated these behaviors may remain with her, but to a lesser extent.

What Are Early Treatment Procedures of the Dietitian?

The early steps in treatment are usually centered on an attempt to change the habit of binging by having the client become more aware of the kind, amount, place, and times of eating. The client is asked to keep a record concerning her attitude about her eating behavior and her re-actions to her "loss of control." As a part of this record, we aks for a report of what she was telling herself as she gorged, of what tastes and smells she was aware, and of what kind of desire or motivation seems to make her continue the binge. she provides a description of the rituals that she uses as to where, when, and how she performs her binges and how she terminates them. These records are brought twice a week to the dietitian who may or may not have the psychologist at the same meeting. In order to better understand what is happening to the client, the client and dietitian attempt to find answers to such questions as the following: Why are some foods eaten more frequently? What are the factors influencing the timing of the binge? What seems to precipitate each episode?

What Type of Meal Planning
Is Done with These Clients?

All meal plans are to be based on the Recommended Dietary Allowances as set up by the Food and Nutrition Board, National Academy of Sciences—National Research Council. This will provide the client with adequate nutrient intake for age and sex, to which the dietitian must calculate any additional or specific nutrient needs for activity and/or medical conditions. Individualization of food patterns also means limiting foods which precipitate binges, dealing with food rituals and fears and providing guidelines in meal planning and preparation. The dietitian should focus attention on helping the client provide herself with nutrients which are appropriate for a "healthy body" rather than allowing the client's obsession with body shape determine intake.

What Is the Next
Phase of Treatment?

Following the recording of these facts and the client's reactions to them, a second phase begins where the client slowly starts to control the timing, amount, and kind of food eaten. Whether she feels hunger or not, she is to eat three or four times a day. While her food choices are not restricted, she is not to eat at any other time. Even if she binges, she is to eat a small meal at the next appropriate meal time. Often a tendency exists for the individual to "punish" herself for a break in restraint by controlling her eating still more diligently after a binge. She may vow to avoid eating for as much as a full day after a binge which of course results in extreme hunger which is often the trigger of another binge. This needs to be avoided by encouraging her to eat at the next meal time "whether you feel hungry or not."

Many women with bulimia tend to "bank" or store the majority of the day's calories until the end of the day in an attempt to either avoid eating them entirely or to avoid having to go to bed hungry. The dietitian will help avoid the banking tendency because this invariably means that the individual will spend a large portion of her day hungry, a condition that promotes out of control eating.

Do Women with Bulimia Resist Forming New Eating Patterns?

The client may object to the proposed format of eating regular meals several times a day because she fears that she will become fat. She will need reassurance from the dietitian that the goal is not to have her gain weight. Remember, the women we are discussing are of normal or above normal body weight. Indeed, to discuss an acceptable range in which the weight may fluctuate as the individual experiments with new eating habits is a wise decision.

Initially, recommending the consumption of four, five, or even six small meals a day may be necessary. Women who vomit regularly experience feelings of fullness or satiety on relatively small amounts of food. Their stomachs also do not empty at a normal rate so that food may stay in their stomachs a long period of time. Consumption of what would be considered a normal meal at one sitting is likely to be difficult for women with bulimia. The problem of delayed gastric emptying and the use of medication to relieve it is covered in the chapter on medical aspects of bulimia.

How Many Calories Are Generally Recommended?

The number of calories to be consumed in a day's time should be sufficient to maintain the woman's body weight. A range of between 1800 to 2400 calories is probably appropriate to achieve this goal. *Under no circumstances is a weight reduction diet appropriate at this time.* Even if the woman is slightly overweight or even obese, this is not the time to consider weight loss. Only after control has been established over the binging/purging behavior and maintained over significant period, should any consideration be made of weight reduction.

Are Relapses Common?

The client must be reassured that relapses are common as she struggles to attain control of her eating behavior. She may need additional support from team members during this period. Encouraging her to try to substitute other activities when the urge to binge starts to develop is important and she should not regard herself as a failure if a relapse does occur.

"GOOD" FOOD, "BAD" FOOD

Do Women with Bulimia Label
Foods as Either Good or Bad?

Women suffering from bulimia frequently have fairly rigid attitudes about food. They may have mentally categorized food into "good" food and "bad" food. Good food is generally low calorie food that they eat when they are in control. Bad food is binge food. This usually consists of high calorie, sweet, or starchy food that the woman regards as forbidden. Sometimes bad food also includes meat because of its relatively high caloric content. The woman is often skeptical when the dietitian explains that her body does not distinguish between the sugar in an orange and the sugar in a doughnut, or between fat in milk and fat in a candy bar. Good food and bad food do not exist. Rather, too much or too little food can be determined. Too much of one kind of food can be eaten and not enough of another to provide a balance, but no food is bad.

Is a Variety of
Foods Recommended?

The patient should be encouraged to include an ever increasing variety of foods in her diet including those previously labeled "bad" food. The dietitian will suggest that a small amount of her favorite binge food be included as "medication" to act as a preventative against the need to binge.

Educating the client is a major factor in the recovery from bulimia. Anyone is more likely to follow suggestions if given a reason or answer. What will this do for me? How does my body respond to "X"? Deficiencies become personalized when the client can see her own behaviors and nutrient deficits? What will happen if I eat? What will happen if I don't eat? Explanation of normal metabolism, digestion and absorption versus altered functioning from inadequate intake allows the client to respond by making wise choices for herself.

The client who is making progress toward overcoming bulimia gradually will begin to unravel the physiology of eating/feeding from the psychology of food selection and will grasp that her health depends on the presence of certain nutrients retained in functioning body cells. The importance of selecting certain categories of foods for her needed nutrients is stressed. Food *groups* such as milk, meat, fruits, vegetables, and bread are used as standards against which the client can begin to organize food choices toward achieving good health. The client is clearly informed that diverting the absorption of calories by vomiting and purging also diverts these necessary nutrients.

**During the Third Phase
of Treatment How Is the
Focus Changed?**

The focus of the sessions now becomes how to have a "healthy body" rather than upon the body's size and shape. Periodically the dietitian explains the dangers of purgatives, diuretics, and vomiting, keeping the client always aware of the risks that she is taking with her behavior.

Follow-up care will need to be continued for at least three months, once a week for the first month, twice a month thereafter. The client's individual needs and progress may dictate a different schedule. Set-backs or resuming bulimic behavior may necessitate longer follow up care.

Treating people with bulimia is a challenging as well as educational experience. Helping people to alter poor eating habits and to observe the physical and emotional benefits from proper nutritional intake has personal rewards for the dietitian. In educating clients, the goal is to create healthy individuals who can function more nearly at full mental and physical capacity.

SUMMARY

To summarize, the client who resolves to make changes in the psychological approach to eating will experience difficult times while doing so. The changes must be approached gradually with the support of the dietitian who has pointed out all the "healthy" food choices the client has been making in her past which require no change. Small, *gradual* additions or subtractions concerning what, when, where, and how often food choice changes might occur are decisions made by the client-dietitian partnership. Lurking in the periphery of the client's decision for change will be the fear of obesity, especially if that individual was once overweight. The dietitian can counsel the client about low calorie substitutions which contain needed nutrients. The trial and error period of change requires agreement and support of dietitian and psychologist.

Gradually through the psychologist, dietitian, and physician's influence the client begins to incorporate into her own thinking the concept of a healthy body, and healthy mind. Her preoccupation with food and body shape gradually make room for concepts of healthy "food," and healthy "body."

ILLUSTRATIVE CASE HISTORY

The case history of Clair which follows is illustrative of many of the points which we have been making in this chapter.

Case of Clair

Clair, a 23 year old college student, had been suffering from bulimia for 4 years when she sought psychological counseling. After making major gains in self-confidence, relationship issues, and working through negative feelings about her body that remained from having been raped at age 20, Clair decided that she was ready to deal with her eating habits. When Clair was referred to a dietitian for nutritional counseling, she described her typical daily food intake. "I eat the same food for breakfast every day—pancakes with no syrup or butter. For lunch I always have a tossed lettuce salad with grated cheese and no dressing. For dinner I usually have a baked potato and cheese with vegetables or a salad. I usually binge once a day, in the late afternoon after I get home from school. I binge on junk food: cookies, ice cream, potato chips, and so forth. I am usually tired and sometimes in negative mood when I binge. Sometimes I am just bored and the eating fills the time. I used to feel very guilty after binging but that is starting to change. I don't feel so guilty any more but I sure would like to get rid of this habit.''

Clair reported her height as 5'3'' and weight at about 103 pounds. Despite the fact that she had no history of obesity and indeed complained of difficulty maintaining her weight at over 100 pounds, Clair expressed the fear that she would become fat if she ever stopped binging and purging. She was small framed and explained, "I am built very much like my mother. She is slightly shorter than I am but she is petite and slim also." Clair complained of feeling tired frequently and of having difficulty getting up in the morning even after eight hours of sleep.

Clair's pattern of severely restricting her food selections is typical of women with bulimia who are attempting to control their binging. A feeling of security emerges when repeating the same meals every day. Clair realized she had gradually narrowed her "good" foods to a very few and regarded all other as "bad." She knew the calorie content of many foods but had little knowledge of how many calories she could consume and maintain her body weight. Like many women with bulimia, she severely underestimated the amount of food she could allow herself and still maintain her weight. Fortunately, Clair had memories of normal eating behavior in her teen years. She could remember when food was something she thought about when she was hungry but spent little time thinking about at other times. There was no "good" food or "bad" food. One of her goals became to return to her pre-bulimia attitudes about food and eating.

Through dietary counseling she was advised to expand her food choices. She was informed that her diet was deficient in protein. She did take a vitamin supplement with iron which she was encouraged to continue. Clair did not consider herself a vegetarian, in spite of the fact that her diet rarely included meat. She agreed to experiment by including chicken and fish in her meals. Although she often ate cheese, she drank little milk. She decided to start drinking milk with some of her meals instead of tea.

As Clair started consuming more protein, she noticed that her energy level was higher and that her fatigue was less noticeable. She was encouraged to eat more for lunch to avoid returning home feeling so very hungry. This helped her reduce the drive to binge in the late *afternoon. At the same time, she was working with her psychologist to develop other methods of dealing with stress and boredom.*

Clair returned to see the dietitian several times to discuss her progress in broadening her meal choices and to ask further questions. Clair was encouraged to start a modest exercise program to improve her muscle tone. She found she now had energy to do this and was pleased with the results.

Client's picture of the number of unresolved issues and feelings she is having while using more and more effort to keep contained.

CHAPTER 14

TECHNICAL ASPECTS
OF
BULIMIA

In this chapter we discuss in more detail material which has been presented briefly elsewhere in the book and is intended for those readers who would like to know more of the details of the mechanism involved in set-point, some of the factors that influence Basal Metabolic Rate, and the affects of aging upon weight.

THE SET-POINT THEORY
OF WEIGHT CONTROL

Recent evidence indicates that the amount of fat deposits contained in the body is pre-set and that this level of body fat is defended by the *central nervous system*. The feeding centers which are located in the *hypothalamus* within the brain adjust to the amount of food eaten in a manner that maintains the body's fat level at a base line which is biologically determined for that individual. This *set-point* varies greatly from person to person and as a result, great individual differences exist among people as to the amount of stored fat that is appropriate for them to carry. Any one individual's base line for what should be considered a healthy weight may be very different from what would be a healthy weight for someone else. Recent information on the relationship between weight and health supports the idea that we have been mislead by the insurance companies' weight charts into a restricted view of what the normal distribution of weight should be (e.g., Bennett & Gurin, 1982).

Keesey (1980) stated that while a great deal of variability exists in weight among humans, a remarkable consistency exists in weight within most individuals over time. Brownell (1982) also noted that the body regulates many of its functions such as body temperature with a great deal of precision. In the case of what a person weighs, so much consistency is maintained that if the average person were to eat a handful of peanuts a day over what the body requires that person would gain 10 pounds of weight a year. Given the consistency with which the body normally maintains a steady weight, we could conclude that each individual has an ideal biological weight controlled by his/her set-point and that for many individuals this natural biological weight will be well above the cultural norms. In fact, in this culture with its particular emphasis on thinness, most people's set-point or the weight they can maintain comfortably, may be considerably above what the culture says is acceptable for them.

The most important feature for us to be aware in thinking about the set-point theory as it relates to the development of bulimia is that an individual's system will defend a certain body weight. This weight may be heavier than the individual wants it to be despite all of the individual's attempts to change it. The individual who is potentially bulimic can probably decrease the size of her fat cells by dieting, but she will not be able to decrease the number of cells to any significant degree. That means that after a period of weight loss, the individual will have the same number of fat cells waiting to be refilled as soon as her restraints fail.

The number of fat cells that an individual possesses is controlled by both heredity and the early nutritional history of the individual (Nisbett, 1972). These two variables that affect the level at which the set-point functions cannot be easily manipulated. This means that women with bulimia and obese persons on a diet are all fighting a battle with their own biological system that never relents. Bennett and Gurin (1982) discussed the attempt of obese persons to overcome their set-point: "It is not a fair contest. The set-point is a tireless opponent. The dieter's only allies are will power and whatever incentives there are that make chronic physical discomfort worthwhile." One of the problems of counseling in the area of eating disorders is the difficulty of bringing people's expectations of what they should weigh into line with what their set-point demands that they should weigh. We need to help individuals to be realistic about how far they can realign their bodies to meet either their own or societal pressures to have a certain look.

Brownell (1982) stated that, "If cure from obesity is defined as reduction to ideal weight and maintenance of that weight for 5 years, a person is more likely to recover from most forms of cancer than from obesity." Other writers are similarly pessimistic about an individual's ability to take off and keep off weight without subjecting their bodies to a great deal of unnecessary stress. When a potentially overweight person ignores the cultural norms and various forms of social pressure and allows his/her weight to go to its set-point, that person behaves like someone who is of normal weight in terms of eating patterns and emotional responses to food (Nisbett, 1972).

The set-point theory holds that the hypothalmic centers of the brain defend different baselines of weight in different individuals. The theory suggests that some very overweight persons could actually be functioning at weight which is under that required by their set-point and that some individuals, who appear to be of normal weight, are also functioning below their set-point. These "normal weight" persons should actually be considered to be underweight and have symptoms of energy deficit. Many of these persons could be said to be in a state of semi-starvation with all of the implications such a condition has for emotional problems and unusual responses to food.

Woods, Decke, and Vasselli (1974) offered some hope for dieters by suggesting that the set-point is somewhat flexible in that a relatively wide range of weight may be possible for any given set-point. Factors which may influence this range of weight are food palatability, food novelty, relative amounts of different sex steroids, and so forth. As we will discuss later, exercise also may be a major factor in resetting this biological thermostat that controls weight.

Let us take a look at bulimia in the context of the previous material to see what evidence we can find in the womens' behavior for the existence of a set-point. Russell (1979), in examining the course of his patients' weight history, found that they were nearly all struggling to maintain a weight which was significantly below what they had weighed before they started their diets. The previous level had evidently been a healthy weight for them even though it sometimes meant they were slightly obese or overweight. He concluded that, "It is clearly the patient's refusal to accept her constitutional weight that leads her to counteract the eating orgies by means of vomiting or purging or both." Pyle, Mitchell, and Eckert (1981) studied the weight changes that took place in women after the onset of bulimia. Weight losses and gains of up to 30 pounds could not be accounted for developmentally. A number of these pateints seemed to cycle between dramatic weight gain and weight loss. This would suggest a battle between the bodies' set-point and the woman's cognitive control system with each taking a turn in the drivers seat.

THE HYPOTHALAMUS

Deep within the brain is a small region called the *hypothalamus.* This has been established as an important management center for coordinating many of the more complex functions of the central nervous system, especially those connected with emotional expression. Its most important function, for the purposes of this book, is its function as the appetite control center. One part of the hypothalamus, the *ventromedial nucleus,* suppresses eating, and another part, the *lateral nucleus,* initiates eating. Another way of looking at it would be to think of the ventromedial nucleus as a weight loss center and the lateral nucleus as a weight gain center. The response of the hypothalamus to sub-optimal weight, that is, weight which is below the individual's set-point, probably plays a major role in the client's attitudes toward food and is influential in bringing on the overeating behavior.

Nisbett (1972) said that the hypothalamus is attuned to the nutritional state of the individual and that messages carried by the blood stream to the hypothalamus influence the hunger response. "It is possible to go further than this and suggest that free fatty acids play an integral role in the ponderostatic mechanism" (Nisbett, 1972, p. 446). He postulated that the hypothalamus monitors the amount of free fatty acids in the bloodstream and responds with a partial shutdown to the presence of excess free fatty acids or some metabolite involved in their production.

His major evidence on this is that obese individuals who behave as if they were hungry even after a full meal have a free fatty acid level which is always and inflexibly high. He hypothesized that if these obese individuals would be allowed to reach their set-point and the free fatty acids brought back into line, the constant hunger would disappear and these people would then eat like normal weight people.

INSULIN-GROWTH HORMONE RATIOS

The discussion of the hypothalamus points up the fact that many things go on regularly in our bodies over which we have little direct control and which exert a powerful influence upon our behavior. For us to achieve even some minimal control over these processes, we need to understand how they work and how they relate to other activities occurring in the body. Another factor, which adds to the complexity of understanding how our set-point works to control our weight, is the *insulin-growth hormone ratio.* Insulin is a protein hormone which is secreted by the beta cells of the islands of Langerhans of the pancreas, an organ which is located behind the lower part of the stomach. Food is digested by the action of insulin which enables nutrition to pass from the bloodstream into the appropriate tissues of the body. The amount of insulin secreted into the bloodstream increases after eating and takes several hours to return to its basal level.

A relationship exists between the insulin-growth hormone ratio and body weight. An alteration of the amount of insulin in the bloodstream will lead to a corresponding change in the amount of growth hormone present. *Growth hormone* is a *protein hormone* secreted by the anterior *pituitary,* a small gland at the base of the brain. Growth hormone is continuously being secreted in basal amounts just as is insulin. The amount secreted covaries with meals, that is, after eating, growth hormone secretion goes down. Obese individuals have low amounts of this hormone in their system. Most of our discussion of the insulin-growth hormone in this section is based upon the work of Woods, Decke, and Vasselli (1974).

Obese individuals normally have elevated levels of basal *insulin*. In addition, when glucose is ingested, they have an increased insulin response; that is, they secrete more insulin than a normal weight person would. Obese children also have a high level of basal insulin. Insulin has an interesting characteristic; it can be produced as a conditioned response without the presence of food. Woods et al. cited evidence that rats that eat for only one two-hour session a day begin to secrete excess insulin at the time of day which has been associated with feeding. Time, not food, has become the cue to cause the secretion of insulin.

Through research studies a correspondence between the insulin-growth hormone ratio and body weight has been established. If one of the hormones increases, the other will make a compensatory decrease. As insulin increases, the growth hormone decreases, and the individual gains weight. As growth hormone increases and insulin decreases, the individual loses weight. These hormones have this effect by influencing the rates of formation and breakdown of stored fat. Woods et al. assumed that the particular ratio which exists between insulin and growth hormone is genetically determined and helps the individual achieve his or her "ideal" weight. Keep in mind that this "ideal" weight for a particular individual may be quite high.

This explanation of weight gain and loss is not inconsistent with the hypothalamus explanation that we gave previously but it gives us another way of understanding how the set-point is activated. Crisp (1981-1982) also used the presence of an increased amount of insulin as an explanation for the continuous eating which occurs in obese individuals. "Meanwhile, any phase of avoidance of dietary carbohydrate promotes changes in carbohydrate metabolism. For instance, the characteristic sustained insulin response that follows an initial ingestion of carbohydrate may itself promote continued ingestion thereafter—the basis of craving for carbohydrates has been generated by abstinence. The individual now eats the box of chocolates having consumed the first one" (Crisp, p. 206).

GENETIC BASIS FOR OVERWEIGHT

When we say that a person is overweight, most of the time we are basing our judgment on a standard which is culturally, not biologically derived. At any particular height a rather wide range of weights is healthy and for the individual genetically normal. That is, the individual whose weight is at the upper end of the normal range may well be functioning at a weight which is consistent with his/her natural propensity. At the risk of sounding redundant, we feel the need to repeat our message that we should expect people to vary in weight around a mean and that just as some people are tall and some are short, some will be heavy and others will be light. Many differences exist among people, which we as a culture do not try to force to fit into preset norms. However, weight seems to be one of those human characteristics that some subgroups, as we saw in our discussion of the media model, insist obey some kind of artificial norm.

In the section on set-point, we established that each individual has a normal weight which may be set by a combination of that individual's genetic makeup and early nutritional history. This weight is maintained by the interaction of a number of biological factors which allow the person to feel comfortable only when he/she is functioning within a limited weight range. The major influence that sets an individual's level of adipose tissue is probably a heredity factor responsible for the number of fat cells with which the person is born.

The mother's eating pattern during pregnancy and the child's early exposure to food also may increase the number of fat cells. Some writers assert that overeating as a baby affects a permanent change in both the number of fat cells and in the size fat deposits. Others suggest that infant overeating is the result of genetic predisposition. Thompson, Jarvie, Lahey, and Cureton (1982), for example, pointed out that children of obese parents expend less energy in the resting state; that is, their basal metabolism is lower and probably more efficient. These children also consume significantly fewer calories per day than did the children of parents who were nonobese. In spite of the fact they eat less, they weigh more, and we are left with a fact which contradicts the common belief that people are fat because they eat too much. We feel that this is evidence for our contention that it may be natural for some babies to be fat.

Much evidence is now in the literature to support this point of view that being fat is not the result of a lack of will power but for many people is biologically preordained (e.g., Woods, Decke, & Vasselli, 1974). This means that many people who are obese are born with a greater than normal number of *adipose* (fat) cells. In one sample, obese subjects were found to have three times as many fat cells as normal weight individuals (Knittle & Hirsch, 1968). As Nisbett (1972) pointed out, starvation and dieting in adults will decrease the size, but not the number, of fat cells to any appreciable degree. After a period of weight loss, the person on a diet still has the same number of fat cells demanding to be filled.

Crisp (1981-1982) believed that this state of semi-starvation also influences those individuals who appear to have a normal, or even a below normal, body weight but are struggling to keep it below a natural adult level. That is, a person whose normal weight might be 125 pounds, but who is holding it down to 110, will have much the same problems as a person whose normal weight would be 250 pounds, but who is holding it down to 210.

Brownell (1982) stated that approximately 25% of all children are overweight by cultural norms (insurance company weight tables not the new ones discussed before). According to the theory that we have discussed previously, the hope that these children will grow up to be slender is likely to be a futile hope. As we have noted previously most people seem to be able to lose weight, but most of those who lose weight do not seem to be able to keep the weight off over any long period of time.

When speaking more specifically of clients with bulimia, Garfinkel et al. (1980) noted that many of clients' mothers were obese (48%). These authors believed this statistic is even more striking when one considers that women who have bulimia tend to be from the upper social classes where a reduced frequency of obesity occurs. Bruch (1973) called these patients thin, fat people because of their personal history of obesity. The evidence shows that many of the women with bulimia have had a problem early in their lives with controlling their weight (e.g., Beumont, George, & Smart, 1976; Russell, 1979; Pyle, Mitchell, & Eckert, 1981). Since they often are at least slightly overweight by cultural standards, at first their efforts to reduce would seem reasonable. Their previous weight, however, was probably healthy for them even if it did amount to what they saw as a degree of obesity. Many of the patients in Pyle's study had had marked fluctuations in their weight after the onset of bulimic behavior, suggesting that they were having a great deal of difficulty holding their weight below their natural level.

The body's natural endeavor to regain weight drives these women to eat more than the average female, because they are in a state of semistarvation. Then, because she is below her natural weight, and because the body has lowered the basal metabolism rate so that she uses food more efficiently, she gains weight more rapidly than a previously nonobese person would by eating the same amounts of food. After the woman has started eating normally and has regained whatever weight she needs to be within her own normal limits, her metabolism will go back to what it was. She will then be able to eat more and not gain weight. From this evidence, we conclude that the client's refusal to accept her constitutional weight is what leads her to begin a pattern in which eating orgies can be easily triggered followed by vomiting and/or purging to get rid of the excess calories.

OVEREATING

In our discussion thus far, two major factors have been stressed which determine a person's natural weight—heredity and early nutritional experiences. In Nisbett's (1972) review of the evidence which led to his conclusions about set-point as a factor in weight control, he reported that available data support the belief that the number of fat cells in an adult are relatively unchangeable. In a comprehensive review of the development of fat cells, Katch and McArdle (1977) came to the conclusion that maybe three, rather than two, critical periods may occur when the number of fat cells increases significantly: the last trimester of pregnancy, the first year of the baby's life, and the adolescent growth spurt. Sjostrom (1980) goes one step further and cites evidence that cell multiplication can occur in adulthood. The number of cells can be increased as a result of overeating. As in the case of cells developed in the other three periods, any increase in the fat cell number cannot be undone by dieting. The increase in fat cells, according to these studies, is permanent. Woods, Decke, and Vasselli (1974) made a similar point, but suggested a different explanation. They proposed that overeating causes an increase in the insulin-growth hormone ratio, that is more insulin and less growth hormone, and this excess insulin in the blood stream leads to increased fat storage and thus increased obesity.

All of this supports the point made earlier that once a person has gained weight during a critical period of development, mechanisms within the individual will seek to perpetuate that weight. The findings of Sjostrom (1980), while interesting, are not necessary to establish this point. Whether or not a person can gain additional fat cells as an adult needs to be researched further. Apparently some people who overeat as they get older increase only the size and not the number of their fat cells. These people can probably lose weight and keep it off if they follow the right program of action. Other people, for whatever reason, increase the number of fat cells. This group will have a great deal of difficulty keeping weight off once it is lost.

A number of other factors also related to the amount eaten still need to be examined. Thompson, Jarvie, Lahey, and Cureton (1982) in their review of studies comparing the amount of food eaten by a group of obese persons and matched sample of normal weight person, found that the overweight individuals did not, as a general rule, eat any more than did their leaner counterparts. The widespread idea that overweight people eat too much was not generally supported. What seemed more likely was that their metabolism was highly effective in the processing of food.

Brownell (1982), on the other hand, believed that obese persons may be cursed by a biology that prefers "fattening" food and by living in a culture that provides unlimited access to these foods. As evidence of this, he cited Sclafani and Springer's (1976) study in the use of a "supermarket diet" consisting of the selection of rich foods which we previously mentioned in Chapter 5. You will probably recall that animals that would ordinarily remain lean, even in the face of abundant food, gained weight when exposed to a sweet, fat rich diet. This brings us back to a social dilemma; we provide individuals with a rich diet and make it as easy as possible for them to eat it, but we put a negative value on the consequences and hold in low esteem individuals who succumb to the attractions of our offerings and gain weight.

We can say a number of things about overeating at this time:

1. not all obese people overeat;

2. some people can make new fat cells when they are older;

3. most people gain the extra fat cells when they are young;

4. the availability of a rich diet is probably a cause of some persons' weight gain; and

5. once the weight is gained, some people will find it impossible to take it off permanently.

AGING AND WEIGHT GAIN

A common observation is that many people tend to get heavier as they get older. The question is, "Is this caused by some natural and biologically based process that is correlated with aging, or is it the result of overeating over a period of time?" In research studies, three factors are reported as causing increased weight in older individuals. The reader is cautioned to keep in mind that these factors probably interact with individual differences, both biological and social; therefore, these factors cannot be expected to produce the same results in all people.

The major factor in weight gain with age appears to be a decline in the *Basal Metabolic Rate (BMR)*. Thompson et al. (1982) cited cross-sectional studies which indicate a reduction in BMR of 3% each decade from age 3 to 80. Longitudinal surveys suggest a more conservative 1 to 2% reduction per decade but agree with the general principle that the BMR declines with age. The decline is associated with an increase in fat and a decrease in the *lean body mass (LBM)*. Some researchers have suggested that the decrease in the number of lean tissue cells is directly responsible for the decrease in BMR since lean tissue cells burn energy at three times the rate of fat cells. In the desirable weight charts issued by the Metropolitan Life Insurance Company for ages 25 to 59 allowances are not made for this steady and seemingly normal increase in weight with age. The Gerontology Research Center of the National Institute of Aging has reanalyzed insurance data to see what the relationship is between weight and mortality. Their conclusions were different from that of Metropolitan in two ways. First, they found no difference in ideal weights between men and women. Second, they found that weights rose with age and felt that a new table was needed that took that fact into consideration. For example, a person, male or female, who is 5'3" tall has a normal range of weight at 20 to 29 years of age of 99 to 131 pounds. At age 50 to 59 that same person's normal range of weight would be from 126 to 158 pounds. An individual who is 5'11" tall would be expected to weigh in the range of 126 to 167 pounds at 20 to 29 years of age and between 172 to 213 pounds at 60 to 69 years of age. This means that many people will naturally develop a higher set-point as they age, resulting in a greater difficulty in losing weight.

Another factor, which helps to explain this increase in weight with age, is that most people decrease the amount of physical activity and exercise as they get older. As physical activity is reduced, weight tends to increase. A third possibility, as yet not fully established, is Sjostrom's (1980) evidence that the number of fat cells can be increased in adulthood and that the increase is a one way street. That is, fat cell numbers will increase but will not decrease. The theory here is that once some individuals have overeaten long enough and filled all of their presently existing fat cells to capacity, they will create new fat cells. On the surface, at least, this is in disagreement with Sim's (1979) finding that most people do not gain fat cells, and they do go back to their normal set-point weight even after they have gained weight. In any case, if we assume along with Sjostrom that at least some individuals do create fat cells following a period of overeating, this would create in them an irreversible condition in which they will not be able to rid themselves of the excess fat cells. Attempts to do so, on the part of these individuals would result in chronic hunger.

UNDERFEEDING-STARVATION

Earlier, we discussed the emotional responses of depression and irritability in individuals who are on a semi-starvation diet (Keys, Brozek, Henschel, Mickelson, & Taylor, 1950). In this same experiment, following the period of semi-starvation, these subjects were allowed to eat as much as they wanted. Not an uncommon occurance was for these men to eat to the point where stomach distention made impossible for them continuing to eat. These men reported that even when they knew they were full, they still felt hungry and wanted to eat more.

Reactions that Keys' subjects reported are similar in some ways to the reactions of women with bulimia in the study by Pyle, Mitchell, and Eckert (1981). These women reported that they had difficulty in knowing when they were full when consuming a normal meal. This problem also was experienced by clients who alternated periods of fasting with periods of binge eating. They typically would fast for nearly 24 hours following a binge, then find themselves so hungry that they could not control their need to eat, thus initiating another binge.

Crisp's (1981-1982) comments on the effects of insulin, which were discussed in the previous section, cast some light on this gorging response resulting from being on a semi-starvation diet. His work suggests a number of steps in the process by which this happens: (1) the avoidance of carbohydrates changes the way in which carbohydrates are metabolized, (2) the avoidance of carbohydrates also contributes to the development of a craving for carbohydrates, (3) eating any carbohydrate produces a sustained insulin response, and (4) this sustained insulin response pushes the individual to further eating. This brings us back to Crisp's conclusion that after eating the first chocolate, the individual now feels driven to eat the whole box.

When we discussed the set-point, we stated that the intensity of the hunger that a particular person feels is related to the nature of the fat cells that he/she possesses. We note that a recent advertisement on TV has a scene where a women is lifted out of bed and, with great speed, carried through the air to the refrigerator where the door opens, and she finds her face in a rich cake. The advertisement is selling a diet pill to sustain an individual through the weak moments which might occur at night. The important message of the advertisement seems to be that without their help, you are likely to fall victim to forces completely beyond your control. Hunger is seen as a monster that has magical powers to take your control away from you.

Keys et al. (1950) found that subjects on a semi-starvation diet were very preoccupied with thoughts of food, taking a great deal of interest in recipe books and pictures of food. Such a preoccupation with food also appears to be the case with clients with bulimia. Pyle et al. (1981) reported that 23 of their 34 patients stated that they enjoyed cooking for others and that they had a positive attitude toward food. These clients frequently took full or part-time jobs as waitresses or food handlers. Some of Russell's (1979) patients volunteered that their minds were filled almost constantly with thoughts of food, so much so that it interfered with their powers of concentration. Overeating, in these patients, was often associated with preoccupations with food. Russell believed that the descriptions of rapid and grotesque eating orgies were in keeping with a failure to achieve normal satiety. Note that this is similar to the behavior of the subjects being rehabilitated from the semi-starvation study.

REFERENCES

Alhibi, R., & McCallum, R.W. (1983). Metoclopramide: Pharmacology and clinical application. *Annals of Internal Medicine, 98,* 86-95.

American Psyciatric Association. (1980). *Diagnostic and statistical manual of mental disorders, 3rd ed. (DSM-III).* Washington, DC: American Psychiatric Assn.

Anderson, W.P., & Bauer, B. (1985). Clients with MMPI high D-Pd: Therapy implications. *Journal of Clinical Psychology, 41,* 181-188.

Bennett, W., & Gurin, J. (1982). *The dieter's dilemma.* New York: Basic Books.

Benson, H., with Klipper, M.Z. (1976). *The Relaxation Response.* New York: Avon.

Beumont, P.J.V., George, G.C.W., & Smart, D.E. (1976). "Dieters" and "Vomiters and purgers" in anorexia nervosa. *Psychological Medicine, 6,* 617-622.

Bo-Lynn, G., Santa-Ana, C.A., Morawski, S.G., & Fordtran, J.S. (1983). Purging and calorie absorption in bulimic patients and normal women. *Annals of Internal Medicine, 99,* 14-17.

Boskind-Lodahl, M. (1976). Cinderella's step-sisters: A feminist perspective on anorexia nervosa and bulimia. *Signs: Journal of Women in Culture and Society, 2,* 342-356.

Brotman, A.W., Herzog, D.B., & Woods, S.W. (1984). Antidepressant treatment of bulimia: The relationship between bingeing and depressive symptomatology. *Journal of Clinical Psychiatry, 45,* 7-9.

Brownell, K.D. (1982). Obesity: Understanding and treating a serious, prevalent, and refractory disorder. *Journal of Consulting and Clinical Psychology, 50,* 820-840.

Brownmiller, S. (1985). *Femininity.* New York: Fawcett Columbine.

Brozek, J., & Erickson, N.K. (1948). Item analysis of the psychoneurotic scales on the Minnesota Multiphasic Personality Inventory in experimental semistarvation. *Journal of Consulting Psychology, 12,* 403-411.

Bruch, H. (1973). *Eating disorders.* New York: Basic Books.

Bruch, H. (1976). *The golden cage.* Cambridge, MA: Harvard University Press.

Bullen, B.A., Skrinar, G.S., Beitins, I.Z., von Mering, G., Turnbull, B.A., & McArthur, J.W. (1985). Induction of menstrual disorders by strenuous exercise in untrained women. *The New England Journal of Medicine, 312,* 1349-1353.

Cohen, S.E., Woods, W.A., & Wyner, J. (1984). Antiemetic efficacy of droperidol and metoclopramide. *Anesthesiology, 60,* 67-69.

Crisp, A.H. (1981-1982). Anorexia nervosa at normal body weight!—The abnormal normal weight control syndrome. *International Journal of Psychiatry in Medicine, 11,* 203-233.

Dally, P., & Gomez, J. (1979). *Anorexia nervosa.* London: Heinemann Medical.

Fairburn, C.G., & Cooper, P.J. (1984). The clinical features of bulimia nervosa. *British Journal of Psychiatry, 144,* 238-246.

Fairburn, C.G. (1985). Cognitive-behavioral treatment for bulimia. In D.M. Garner and P.E. Garfinkel (Eds.). *Anorexia Nervosa & Bulimia,* New York: Guilford Press.

Garfinkel, P., & Garner, D. (1982). *Anorexia nervosa: A multidimensional perspective.* New York: Brunner/Mazel.

Garfinkel, P.E., Moldofsky, H., & Garner, D.M. (1980). The heterogeneity of anorexia nervosa: Bulimia as a distinct subgroup. *Archives of General Psychiatry, 37,* 1036-1040.

Garner, D.M., Garfinkel, P.E., Schwartz, D., & Thompson, M. (1980). Cultural expectations of thinness in women. *Psychological Reports, 47,* 483-491.

Garrow, J.S. (1978). *Energy balance and obesity in man* (2nd ed.). Amsterdam: Elsevier.

Gordon, T., & McKay, G. (1970). *Parent effectiveness training: The tested new way to raise a responsible child.* New York: Wyden Books.

Green, R.S., & Rau, J.H. (1974). Treatment of compulsive eating disturbances with anticonvulsant medication. *American Journal of Psychiatry, 131,* 428-432.

Green, R.S., & Rau, J.H. (1977). The use of diphenylhydantoin in compulsive eating disorders: Further studies. In R.A. Vigersky (Ed.), *Anorexia nervosa.* New York: Raven Press.

Halmi, K.A., Falk, J.R., & Schwartz, E. (1981). Binge-eating and vomiting: A survey of a college population. *Psychological Medicine, 11,* 697-706.

Hamburger, W.W. (1951). Emotional aspects of obesity. *Medical Clinics of North America, 35,* 483-499.

Harris, R.T. (1983). Bulimarexia and related serious eating disorders with medical complications. *Annals of Internal Medicine, 99,* 800-807.

Hatsukami, D., Owen, P., Pyle, R., & Mitchell, J. (1982). Similarities and differences on the MMPI between women with bulimia and women with alcohol or druge abuse problems. *Addictive Behaviors, 7,* 435-439.

Herman, C.P., & Mack, D. (1975). Restrained and unrestrained eating. *Journal of Personality, 42,* 647-660.

Herman, C.P., & Polivy, J. (1975). Anxiety, restraint, and eating behavior. *Journal of Abnormal Psychology, 84,* 666-672.

Hillard, J.R., & Hillard, P.J.A. (1984). Anorexia nervosa, and diabetes—deadly combinations. *Psychiatria Clinica, 7,* 367-379.

Hsu, L.K.G. (1984). Treatment of bulimia with Lithium. *American Journal of Psychiatry, 141,* 1260-1262.

Hudson, J.I., Pope, H.G., Jonas, J.M., & Yurgelun-Todd, D. (1983). Family history study of anorexia nervosa and bulimia. *British Journal of Psychiatry, 142,* 133-138.

Huenemann, R.L., Shapiro, L.R., Hampton, M.C., & Mitchell, B.W. (1966). A longitudinal study of gross body composition and body conformation and their association with food and activity in a teenage population. *American Journal of Clinical Nutrition, 18,* 325-38.

Katch, F.I., & McArdle, W.D. (1977). *Nutrition, weight control, and exercise.* Boston: Houghton Mifflin.

Keesey, R.E. (1980). A set-point analysis of the regulation of body weight. In A.J. Stunkard (Ed.), *Obesity.* Philadelphia, PA: Saunders.

Keys, A., Brozek, J., Henschel, A., Mickelson, D., & Taylor, H. (1950). *The biology of human starvation.* Minneapolis: University of Minnesota Press.

Knittle, J.L., & Hirsch, J. (1968). Effect of early nutrition on the development of rat epididymal fat pads: Cellularity and metabolism. *Journal of Clinical Investigation, 47,* 2091.

Landorf, J. (1982). *Irregular people.* Waco, TX: Word Books.

Love, S., & Johnson, C. (1985). Etiological factors in the development of bulimia. *Nutrition News, 48,* 5.

Mayer, J., Roy, P., & Mitra, K.P. (1956). Relation between caloric intake, body weight, and physical work. *American Journal of Clinical Nutrition, 4,* 169-75.

Miller, P.M., & Sims, K.L. (1981). Evaluation and component analysis of a comprehensive weight control program. *International Journal of Obesity, 5,* 57-66.

Mitchell, J.E., & Groat, R. (1984). A placebo-controlled, double-blind trial of Amitriptylene in bulimia. *Journal of Clinical Psychopharmacology, 4,* 186-193.

Mitchell, J.E., Hatsukami, D., Goff, G., Pyle, R.L., Eckert, E.D., & Davis, L.E. (1985). Intensive outpatient group treatment for bulimia. In D.M. Garner and P.E. Garfinkel (Eds.), *Anorexia nervosa & bulimia.* New York: Guilford Press.

Mitchell, J.E., Pyle, R.L., & Eckert, E.D. (1981). Frequency and duration of binge-eating episodes in patients with bulimia. *American Journal of Psychiatry, 138,* 487-488.

Nisbett, R.E. (1972). Hunger, obesity, and the ventromedial hypothalamus. *Psychological Review, 79,* 433-453.

Nogami, Y., & Yabana, F. (1977). On Kibarashi-gui (binge eating). Folia Psychiatrica et Neurologica. *Japonica, 31,* 159-66.

Polivy, J., & Herman, C.P. (1976). Clinical depression and weight change: A complex relation. *Journal of Abnormal Psychology, 85,* 338-340.

Polivy, J., & Herman, C.P. (1985). Dieting and bingeing: A causal analysis. *American Psychologist, 40,* 193-201.

Pope, H.G., Hudson, J.T., Jonas, J.M., & Yurgelun-Todd, D. (1983). Bulimia treated with Imipramine: A placebo-controlled, double blind study. *American Journal of Psychiatry, 140,* 554-558.

Pope, H.G., & Hudson, J.I. (1984). *New hope for binge eaters.* New York: Harper & Row.

Pyle, R.L., Mitchell, J.E., & Eckert, E.D. (1981). Bulimia: A report of 34 cases. *Journal of Clinical Psychiatry, 42*(2), 60-65.

Rigotti, N.A., Nussbaum, S.R., Herzog, D.B., & Neer, R.M. (1984). Osteoporosis in women with anorexia nervosa. *New England Journal of Medicine, 311,* 1601-1606.

Russell, G.F.M. (1979). Bulimia nervosa: An ominous variant of anorexia nervosa. *Psychological Medicine, 9,* 429-448.

Saleh, J.W., & Lebwohl, P. (1980). Metoclopramide-induced gastric emptying in patients with anorexia nervosa. *American Journal of Gastroenterology, 74,* 127-132.

Schachter, S. (1971). Some extraordinary facts about obese humans and rats. *American Psychologist, 26,* 129-144.

Sclafani, A., & Springer, D. (1976). Dietary obesity in adult rats. *Physiology and Behavior, 17,* 461-471.

Sharkey, B.J. (1975). *Physiological Fitness and Weight Control.* Missoula, MT: Mountain Press.

Sims, E.A.H. (1979). Definitions, criteria, and prevalence of obesity. In G.A. Bray (Ed.), *Obesity in America.* Washington, DC: U.S. Government Printing Office, pp. 20-36. (DHEW Publication No. NIH 79-559).

Sjostrom, L. (1980). Fat cells and body weight. In A.J. Stunkard (Ed.), *Obesity.* Philadelphia, PA: Saunders.

Stewart, J.W., Walsh, T., Wright, L., Roose, S.P., & Glassman, A.H. (1984). An open trial of MAO inhibitors in bulimia. *Journal of Clinical Psychiatry, 45,* 217-219.

Story, M. (1984). Adolescent life-style and eating behavior. In K. Mahan & J.M. Rees, *Nutrition in adolescence.* Times Mirror/Mosby.

Strober, M., Salkin, B., Burroughs, J., & Morrell, W. (1982). Validity of the bulimia-restricter distinction in anorexia nervosa. *Journal of Nervous and Mental Disease, 170,* 345-351.

Thompson, J.K., Jarvie, G.J., Lahey, B.B., & Cureton, K.J. (1982). Exercise and obesity: Etiology, physiology, and intervention. *Psychological Bulletin, 91,* 55-79.

Walsh, T., Stewart, J.W., Wright, L., Harrison, W., Roose, S.P., & Glassman, A.H. (1982). *American journal of Psychiatry, 139,* 1629-1630.

Wardle, J. (1980). Dietary restraint and binge eating. *Behavioral Analysis and Modification, 4,* 201-209.

Wardle, J., & Beinart, H. (1981). Binge eating: A theoretical review. *British Journal of Clinical Psychology, 20,* 97-109.

Wermuth, B.M., Davis, K.L., Hollister, L., & Stunkard, A.J. (1977). Phenytoin treatment of the binge-eating syndrome. *American Journal of Psychiatry, 134,* 1249-1253.

Williamson, D.A., Kelley, M.L., Davis, C.J., Ruggiero, L., & Blouin, D.C. (1985). Psychopathology of eating disorders: A controlled comparison of bulimic, obese, and normal subjects. *Journal of Consulting and Clinical Psychology, 53,* 161-166.

Wolcott, R.B., Yager, J., & Gordon, G. (1984). Dental sequelae to the binge-purge syndrome (Bulimia): Report of cases. *Journal of the American Dental Association, 109,* 723-725.

Woods, S.C., Decke, E., & Vasselli, J.R. (1974). Metabolic hormones and regulation of body weight. *Psychological Review, 81,* 26-43.

Wooley, O.W., & Dyrenforth, S.R. (1979). Theoretical, practical, and social issues in behavioral treatments of obesity. *Journal of Applied Behavior Analysis, 12,* 3-26.

INDEX

CONTENT

CONTENT INDEX

leader qualifications 108
new members 110-1, 112
screening 108-11
support 118-9
telephone calls 120

H

Habits, eating 158
Headache
neurological symptoms 19
Health 155-69
Health problems
effects 70
Height effect
tall 69-70
Hemorrhoids 18
Hormone
growth 176
insulin-growth ratio 175-6
protein 176
Hunger 57-8
Hypercalcemia 21
Hypercholesterolemia 21
Hypermagnesemia 21
Hypertriglyceridemia 21
Hypocalcemia 20
Hypokalemia 20
cardiac dysrhythmias 18
gastrointestinal 18
kidney tubules 18
renal 18
Hyponatremia 21
Hypothalamus 172, 174-5

I

Ideal body shape
recent evolution 39
Imagery exercise 93-4
Imipramine 24
Individual differences 27-33

Information gathering 75-7
Insulin 175-7
effects of 183
Insulin-growth hormone ratios 175-7
Ipecac 20
Irregular people 129-32
Irritability 53
Issues
emotional 143
personal 115-7
recovery 145-53

J

Jan, case of 1-3, 42-3
Jane, case of 9-10
Jill, case of 94-6
Journal, keeping a 89, 98

K

Karen, case of 15, 32-3
Kathy, letter by 123-4

L

Lateral nucleus 174-5
Laurie, case of 22-3
Laxative 20
Leader, qualifications 108
Lean body mass (LBM) 103, 182
Letter
Kathy 123-4
Lithium 24

M

Magical thinking 85-6

R

Recovery
affect the need to eat 147
coping skill for binge 148-9
issues 145-53
retaining food 148
significant others interfere 150-1
time span between sessions 152-3
views of others 152
what constitutes 146
Reflux esophagitis 18
Reframe 81
Reframe the behavior 79
Relapses 149-50, 164
prescribing 151
Relaxation exercise 91-3
Relaxation training 89, 91-4
Renal
hypokalemia 18
Reproductive system
affects on 18
delayed menarche 21
infertility 21
normal menstrual bleeding 21
secondary amenorrhea 21
Response to food
persons differ 45
Responses, emotional
to dieting 49-58
Restraint-binge-purge cycle 56
Rewards
emotionally anethesized 89
for binging 88-9
Right way 66
Rita, case of 31
Ruth, case of 60

S

Schizophrenia 28
Self esteem 145-6
Self-criticism 114-5

commonality 114
Self-denial of success 115
Self-induced vomiting 19-20
alimentary tract 19
heart 19
pulmonary system 19
renal system 19
Semi-starvation 50, 178
dieting 50
Set-point 28-9, 177, 183-4
concept 29
functioning below 45-7
regulate calorie intake 54-5
theory 172-4
weight control 172-4
Sexual traumas 117
Sharon, case of 22-3
Sherri, case of 14-15
Siblings 138
troubles with 115-7
Skills, coping
alternate list 149
performing a task 148
Skills, decision-making 96-8
Social contacts 120-1
Starvation, underfeeding 183-4
Stomach emptying 18
STOP sign 90-1
Stress
effective method 88-9
trigger for overeating 56
weight control 7-8
Structure 111-2
group sessions 111-2
Suicide
attempts 24, 52
ideation 24
Support
group members 118-9
Syndrome
clinical 16-17

T

Task

INDEX

NAME

NAME INDEX

A

Alhibi, R. 23, 185
American Psychiatric Association
6, 185
Anderson, W.P. 51, 185

B

Bauer, B. 51, 185
Beinart, H. 30, 45, 46, 51, 57,
104, 189
Beitins, I.Z. 21, 185
Bennett, W. 172, 173, 185
Benson, H. 91, 185
Beumont, P.J.V. 53, 179, 185
Blouin, D.C. 36, 189
Bo-Lynn, G. 76, 87, 185
Boskind-Lodahl, M. 43, 185
Brotman, A.W. 24, 185
Brownell, K.D. 30, 103, 172, 173,
178, 180, 185
Brownmiller, S. 68, 185
Brozek, J. 50, 183, 185, 187
Bruch, H. 43, 54, 55, 178, 185
Bullen, B.A. 21, 185
Burroughs, J. 50, 189

C

Cohen, S.E. 23, 186
Cooper, P.J. 15, 17, 186
Crisp, A.H. 42, 44, 52, 53, 177, 178,
183, 186
Cureton, K.J. 39, 103, 177, 180,
189

D

Dally, P. 57, 186
Davis, C.J. 36, 189
Davis, K.L. 23, 189
Davis, L.E. 25, 187
Decke, E. 29, 174, 176, 178, 180,
189

Dyrenforth, S.R. 30, 189

E

Eckert, E.D. 16, 25, 43, 174, 179,
183, 187, 188
Erickson, N.K. 50, 185

F

Fairburn, C.G. 15, 17, 52, 53, 186
Falk, J.R. 6, 186
Fordtran, J.S. 76, 87, 185

G

Garfinkel, P. 36, 43, 52, 53, 186,
187
Garner, D. 36, 43, 52, 186, 187
Garrow, J.S. 30, 186
George, G.C.W. 53, 179, 185
Glassman, A.H. 24, 188, 189
Goff, G. 25, 187
Gomez, J. 57, 186
Gordon, G. 19, 189
Gordon, T. 141, 186
Green, R.S. 23, 186
Groat, R. 24, 187
Gurin, J. 172, 173, 185

H

Halmi, K.A. 6, 186
Hamburger, W.W. 56, 58, 186
Hampton, M.C. 38, 187
Harris, R.T. 17, 186
Harrison, W. 24, 189
Hatsukami, D. 17, 24, 25, 51, 186,
187
Henschel, A. 50, 183, 187
Herman, C.P. 6, 46, 54, 186, 187, 188
Herzog, D.B. 21, 24, 185, 188
Hillard, J.R. 70, 187
Hillard, P.J.A. 70, 187
Hirsch, J. 178, 187

Hollister, L. 23, 189
Hsu, L.K.G. 187
Hudson, J.I. 24, 50, 52, 187, 188
Huenemann, R.L. 38, 187

J

Jarvie, G.J. 39, 103, 177, 180, 188
Johnson, C. 159, 187
Jonas, J.M. 24, 50, 187, 188

K

Katch, F.I. 106, 179, 187
Keesey, R.E. 172, 187
Kelley, M.L. 36, 189
Keys, A. 50, 51, 53, 55, 183, 184, 187
Klipper, M.Z. 91, 185
Knittle, J.L. 178, 187

L

Lahey, B.B. 39, 103, 177, 180, 188
Landorf, J. 129, 132, 187
Lebwohl, P. 16, 23, 188
Love, S. 159, 187

M

Mack, D. 46, 186
Mayer, J. 104, 187
McArdle, W.D. 106, 179, 187
McArthur, J.W. 21, 185
McCallum, R.W. 23, 185
McKay, G. 141, 186
Mickelson, D. 50, 183, 187
Miller, P.M. 103, 187
Mitchell, B.W. 38, 187
Mitchell, J. 16, 17, 24, 25, 43, 51, 174, 179, 183, 186, 187, 188
Mitra, K.P. 104, 187
Moldofsky, H. 43, 186
Morawski, S.G. 76, 87, 185
Morrell, W. 50, 188

N

Neer, R.M. 21, 188
Nisbett, R.E. 30, 52, 57, 173, 175, 178, 179, 188
Nogami, Y. 51, 188
Nussbaum, S.R. 21, 188

O

Owen, P. 17, 24, 51, 186

P

Polivy, J. 6, 46, 54, 187, 188
Pope, H.G. 24, 50, 52, 187, 188
Pyle, R. 16, 17, 24, 25, 43, 51, 56, 174, 179, 183, 186, 187, 188

R

Rau, J.H. 23, 186
Rigotti, N.A. 21, 188
Roose, S.P. 24, 188, 189
Roy, P. 104, 187
Ruggiero, L. 36, 189
Russell, G.F.M. 42, 52, 174, 179, 184, 188

S

Saleh, J.W. 16, 23, 188
Salkin, B. 50, 189
Santa-Ana, C.A. 76, 87, 185
Schachter, S. 45, 188
Schwartz, D. 36, 186
Schwartz, E. 6, 186
Sclafani, A. 58, 188
Shapiro, L.R. 38, 187
Sharkey, B.J. 103, 188
Sims, E.A.H. 182, 188
Sims, K.L. 103, 187
Sjostrom, L. 180, 182, 188
Skrinar, G.S. 21, 185
Smart, D.E. 53, 179, 185

Springer, D. 58, 188
Stewart, J.W. 24, 188, 189
Story, M. 159, 160, 188
Strober, M. 50, 189
Stunkard, A.J. 23, 189

T

Taylor, H. 50, 183, 187
Thompson, J.K. 39, 103, 104, 106, 176, 180, 188
Thompson, M. 36, 186
Turnbull, B.A. 21, 185

V

Vasselli, J.R. 29, 174, 176, 178, 180, 189
von Mering, G. 21, 185

W

Walsh, T. 24, 188, 189
Wardle, J. 30, 43, 45, 46, 51, 57, 104, 189
Wermuth, B.M. 23, 189
Williamson, D.A. 36, 51, 189
Wolcott, R.B. 19, 189
Woods, S.C. 29, 174, 176, 178, 180, 189
Woods, S.W. 24, 185
Woods, W.A. 23, 186
Wooley, O.W. 30, 189
Wright, L. 24, 188, 189
Wyner, J. 23, 186

Y

Yabana, F. 51, 188
Yager, J. 19, 189
Yurgelun-Todd, D. 24, 50, 187, 188

ABOUT
THE
AUTHORS

Wayne Anderson has a Ph.D. in psychology from the University of Missouri at Columbia and is presently Chair of the Joint Training Program in Counseling Psychology. He has a dual appointment at the University of Missouri as a professor of psychology and as a Counseling Psychologist with the Counseling Services. Previously he worked with VA psychiatric hospitals for seven years. He is presently involved with the Columbia Police Department as an instructor to officers on dealing with anger, stress, and problem citizens. His research interests are the psychology of the aggressive offender (murder and rape) and the effects of counselor self-disclosure upon client behavior. Dr. Anderson has published over 70 articles and book chapters on various aspects of psychology.

Barbara Bauer has a Ph.D. in psychology from the University of Missouri at Columbia and is presently in private practice at the Center for Individual and Family Counseling in Columbia, Missouri. Her practice consists primarily of young women with eating disorders. She developed an interest in working with women with builimia while an intern at the Counseling Services at the University of Missouri. While interning, she was responsible for setting up the group treatment program for bulimia at the Columbia campus. In addition to her work with bulimia, she also consults with the Columbia Police Department as an instructor and works individually with officers involved in stressful incidents.

Robert W. Hyatt, M.D., is in the private practice of Internal & Adolescent Medicine in Columbia, Missouri. He is Assistant Clinical Professor of Medicine in the Department of Family & Community Medicine at the University of Missouri at Columbia.

He was graduated from the University of Missouri at Columbia with a B.A., where he attended medical school and completed his internship and residency in Internal Medicine. He completed a fellowship in Adolescent Medicine at Children's Hospital of Los Angeles (USC) and began private practice in Columbia in 1976.

He is a member of the Society of Adolescent Medicine (both national and Mid-West Regional Chapter). He is a member of the American College of Physicians, the American Society of Internal Medicine, and the American Medical Association.